4-50

PROVIDENCE AND EVIL

To the dear and honoured memory of

L. G. SARGENT

Hereafter, in a better world than this,
I shall desire more love and knowledge of you.

PROVIDENCE AND EVIL

THE STANTON LECTURES 1971–2

PETER GEACH

Professor of Logic, University of Leeds

CAMBRIDGE UNIVERSITY PRESS

CAMBRIDGE

LONDON · NEW YORK · MELBOURNE

Published by the Syndics of the Cambridge University Press
The Pitt Building, Trumpington Street, Cambridge CB2 1RP
Bentley House, 200 Euston Road, London NW1 2DB
32 East 57th Street, New York, NY 10022, USA
296 Beaconsfield Parade, Middle Park, Melbourne 3206,
Australia

First published 1977

Printed in Great Britain by
Western Printing Services Ltd, Bristol

Library of Congress Cataloguing in Publication Data
Geach, Peter Thomas
Providence and Evil
(Stanton lectures; 1971-2)
1. Theodicy – Addresses, essays, lectures
I. Title. II. Series
BT160.G3   231'.8   76-28005
ISBN 0 521 21477 7

ANALYTICAL TABLE OF CONTENTS

Introduction

v

is always true if 'so-and-so' is short for a logically consistent description of a feat; (3) that if 'God does so-and-
so' is logically possible, then 'God can do so-and-so' is
true; (4) that if 'God *will* do so-and-so' is logically consistent, 'God can do so-and-so' is true. I discuss these
senses in order.

(1) God has been believed to be absolutely omnipotent
– able to override logic – by Descartes and by many
naive Christians. And unscrupulous logicians could fadge
up a case for this view. But we cannot say anything
coherent about a supposed supra-logical God.

(2) We must distinguish between self-contradictory
descriptions and mere gibberish; and as logicians know,
proofs of consistency are sometimes hard to come by.

'God can bring about everything that God can bring
about' is obviously true only in one sense; in another
reading this expresses a self-contradiction.

Lying and promise-breaking are logically possible feats
that Christians cannot hold to be possible for God. And
making a thing which its maker cannot destroy is a
logically possible feat, a feat some creatures do perform;
but whether we say that God cannot perform this feat
or that he can, there turns out to be *some* logically
possible feat which God cannot perform.

(3) Even when 'So-and-so is done' is not self-contradictory, 'God does so-and-so' may be; so the third
sense of 'omnipotent' is weaker than the second. But the
third sense likewise is not maintainable; for even if 'God
brings it about that so-and-so never happens' is logically
consistent, 'God *can* bring it about that so-and-so never

So all the four senses of 'omnipotent' we have considered turn out to involve both inherent logical difficulties and consequences fatal to Christian faith. But these are not difficulties against the doctrine that God is *almighty* in the sense I explained. Aquinas's list of things we may not say God can do shows that Aquinas could not consistently ascribe to God omnipotence in any of our four senses.

But Aquinas's list raises another difficulty: he says God *cannot* do a number of things that God incarnate *did*, according to Christian belief. The solution of this difficulty would involve distinguishing between what God *as God* can do and what God the Son can do *as man*. We use such 'as' propositions in ordinary life quite often; but our understanding of their logic is hardly better than Aristotle's.

Chapter 2: *An Irrelevance of Omnipotence*

Hostile critics of Christian faith often hold *both* that Christians are committed to a logically incoherent doctrine of omniscience *and* that Christians are faced with the problem of reconciling God's omnipotence with the world's evil. This criticism fails if we hold that the doctrine of omnipotence – of God's being able to do everything – is indeed incoherent, but that Christians are not bound to hold it. But I have argued that Christians are bound to hold that God is *almighty*; this raises a genuine problem of evil.

What God can do *simpliciter* is what he can do in the

Analytical Table of Contents

Chapter 3: Omniscience and the Future

The simple rule about God's knowledge is given by the formula: God knows that p if and only if p. This holds *whatever* proposition 'p' represents. If 'p' is short for a tensed proposition like 'Hitler is alive', 'God knows that p' will cease to be true when 'p' ceases to be true; but Aquinas was right in holding that this involves no real change in God's mind.

God cannot know everything by seeing all history as an unchanging pattern, because history is not an unchanging pattern.

We cannot give an otherwise senseless form of words sense by prefacing it with 'God knows that...' or 'God knows whether...' We must know how to talk sense about the future before trying to talk about God's knowledge of the future.

To talk sense about the future, we must understand prevention. There are no identifiable individuals prevented from coming into being. What is prevented is always something that was going to happen.

If something did in fact happen, we may not infer that it *always* was going to happen. By reason of some preventive action, what is now going to happen may differ from what was previously going to happen.

'If Jones is going to be hanged, nobody was ever able to prevent Jones being hanged' is ambiguous; there are two ways of taking it that bring it out trivially true; but in a third sense it is obviously false, as we all in practice assume.

responsible for it, like a man watching a murder from a high tower.

It has no clear sense to say God causes the act of sin but not its sinfulness; and we are not related to God as fictional characters are to their author.

We may, however, expect problems about sin to be irresoluble *for us*, just because we are sinners: even as a man of confused mind is not better but worse qualified to sort out other people's confusions.

A Christian will say that sin is permitted because there are certain forms of virtue which logically could not exist if sin did not.

Chapter 4: Animal Pain

Sin, not pain, gives rise to the really serious problem of evil.

But we must not ignore the magnitude and duration of pain in the animal world: C. S. Lewis's attempts to mitigate the difficulty appear sophistical.

Lewis's suggestion that predatory and parasitic forms of life are due to diabolical interference with evolution could not remove God's responsibility for letting the Devil act thus.

God must not be conceived as ordaining a broad plan of evolution without responsibility for the unfortunate results to individual beings.

Teleological explanation does not mean explanation by the occurrence of some event of desire or planning in some mind. Desire and will are to be analysed in terms

Analytical Table of Contents

Ought God to be expected to have virtues like ours? Some human virtues can be ascribed in a transferred sense to God; but many virtues, e.g. chastity and courage, cannot be ascribed to God.

God should be loved and adored for his great glory, because he is all truth and all beauty: not because of his sharing all the moral virtues of his creatures.

Sympathy with the lower animals is a virtue in men because we have some community of nature with them. But it is a virtue only if moderated by an Aristotelian mean. The Divine Nature is not animal, and sympathy with the pains of animals could be no virtue in God.

'Being men, we can only judge God by human standards' is sophistically ambiguous.

We must submit in utter obedience to the Divine Power, because this is the power of Truth. Such submission can give men strength to defy tyrants, in confidence that God reigns.

Chapter 5: Original Sin

When people say the Christian story is irrelevant to modern man, what they often have in mind is a denatured Christianity that omits the doctrine of the Fall.

This doctrine was for long accepted by all Christians, and the claim was that God inspired this teaching. If we accept the claim, that settles the matter. If we reject it, we may perhaps follow the world's conjectures about man's origin and destiny; but we should be very foolish

Analytical Table of Contents

The doctrine of the Virgin Conception is congruous in the light of this.

Christians ought to wish each man salvation from that natural condition which the will of unconverted men approves. Salvation is individual; a branch from the rotten tree can live only if cut off and grafted on a healthy tree.

Chapter 6: The Ordainer of the Lottery

We all have to fight against evil; we need a sound view of what is actual and what is possible in order that we may fight well.

Nobody has to burden himself with all the evil in the world as if *he* were guilty of it all.

Some concern about the pains of animals is ill-regulated; and there is no such sin as 'disturbing the balance of Nature'.

Because of Original Sin, we must act like doctors giving palliative treatment to a chronically and incurably ill patient, and be sceptical of any large-scale schemes to better man's condition.

It does not take Christian belief to recognize the evils Christians ascribe to Original Sin. There is no hope of a remedy, unless the Judaeo-Christian Messianic hope is warranted.

Why are people made to suffer indiscriminately? Hobbes toughly replied that God's almightiness was justification enough for this. This answer is far less

and evils of fortune distributed according to the laws of chance. The Ordainer of the lottery lets us know its terms; his justice in respect of the lottery consists only in playing fair. In this life the results of the lottery often overshadow the natural rewards and penalties of our conduct.   I

God's justice cannot consist in rendering equal good to equals; men are not all equal, and to say they are all equal 'in God's sight' is profane clap-trap. Nor does God promise to all men an equal chance of an equal share in grace and glory. But it is enough that for every man without exception there is a way of gaining the everlasting joys of Heaven.   I

Chapter 7: Hell

If we know anything at all of Christ's teaching, we know that it included the doctrine that many men are irretrievably lost.   I

We need God, but God does not need us. God has nothing to gain from us; but he cannot wish for us a permanent happiness independent of him; no such thing is possible.   I

God desires human freedom, not the greatest happiness of the greatest number. Wicked men are unwittingly used to shape the virtue of the just. Immortality is a gratuitous gift: we could glorify God even if he had made us mortal. Perhaps some other rational creatures have perished for ever by their own folly.   I

Our hope of immortality is a hope of resurrection.   I

of the line of time, and that after the fork two alternative futures are *both* realized; one for the blessed, one for the damned. For the damned, heavenly bliss is something that was going to be but will now never be; and so is it also for the blessed as regards the pains of Hell.

Phrases like 'the next world' originally referred to an age, not to a place; it is congruous with this to think of the separation of the damned from the blessed as temporal rather than spatial.

The damned will not acknowledge God's Justice, but perforce will submit to his Power; their fate is irreversible because time is irreversible. And the inanimate creatures, which now are so to say unwillingly subject to man's perverse wills, will no longer be obedient, but will continually frustrate and enrage the wicked. This will not be a special infliction, but the ending of a miraculous mercy.

Nobody incurs such a dreadful fate except by his own fault. Let us hope rather to be among those who live in the age when 'the wicked shall not be'.

Appendix. It is logically possible that an unending series of miseries all occur in a finite time. In that case though the damned might truly say 'This will never end', the Saints could one day truly say 'Thank God that's over.'

PREFACE

This volume contains all but one of the eight Stanton
Lectures delivered in 1971–2. The first lecture was on
metaphysical dogmas, their importance for religion, and
the grounds for accepting them: it took the form of a
commentary on the first two chapters of McTaggart's
Some Dogmas of Religion. This will have prepared the
ground for the whole three-year course, by bringing out
some general aspects of my thoughts in the philosophy of
religion, and in particular the pervasive influence of
McTaggart upon me; but upon consideration I thought
it did not fit into a unity with the other seven lectures,
so I reserve it for a forthcoming work on McTaggart's
philosophy.

I had the good luck to be asked to redeliver this course
at Calvin College, Grand Rapids, Michigan. The chance
to share my problems with Alvin Plantinga, Anthony
Kenny and Terence Penelhum was very valuable, all the
more because I could attend their own courses of lectures.

I am very grateful to the University of Cambridge for
inviting me to give these lectures, to Donald MacKinnon
for his unfailing support, and to Calvin College for
organizing the occasion of their redelivery and for much
hospitality. Finally, I warmly thank the Master and Fellows of St John's College Cambridge for taking a son of
Balliol under their wing and being my very generous

hosts, not only for the three years of the Stanton Lectures, but during the year's leave of absence kindly given me by the University of Leeds in the year 1974–5.

The first two chapters of this book have been printed as articles in *Philosophy* Vol. 48 and are here republished by kind permission of the editor.

P. T. GEACH

INTRODUCTION

Providence as ascribed traditionally to God includes both almighty power over the world and complete knowledge of all that is in the world and all possible future developments. These attributes are clearly ascribed to God in the Scriptures and in Jewish and Christian tradition; and not there alone, for Anaxagoras for example said of his *Nous*, the Mind which made the cosmos, that it has power over all other things, but is not mixed up with them so that they can react upon it, and that it has complete knowledge of past, present, and future. It is the assertion that the world is ruled by Divine Providence that gives rise to the problem of evil; if the world is planned in all its detail by a mind, can that mind be called good, given the world's actual nature?

I shall begin by examining some problems about the attributes of almighty power and omniscience. I then turn to various forms of evil in the world. I begin with the problem of animal pain; for many modern people, inflicting unnecessary suffering is the very type of iniquity, and what suffering could it ever be necessary for an almighty and omniscient being to inflict on beings incapable of sin? Next, I consider the doctrine of Original Sin: I argue that this doctrine cannot be abandoned without the total destruction of Christian belief, and that its negative side, the radical corruption of the human will, is something that we are pretty well compelled to accept even apart from revelation; what revelation offers is some hope of relief from this desperate situation. Then I consider the evidence that in this life good and evil fortune are distributed by the laws of chance, not by desert, and the consequences for our view of Divine Justice. Finally, I consider whether we ought to reject the *prima facie* evidence that men can irretrievably ruin themselves by folly and vice; and I argue that such final ruin is not excluded by the goodness of God; not even if this means that many men turn God's gift of immortality into an endless misery for themselves.

I

OMNIPOTENCE

It is fortunate for my purposes that English has the two words 'almighty' and 'omnipotent', and that apart from any stipulation by me the words have rather different associations and suggestions. 'Almighty' is the familiar word that comes in the creeds of the Church; 'omnipotent' is at home rather in formal theological discussions and controversies, e.g. about miracles and about the problem of evil. 'Almighty' derives by way of Latin '*omnipotens*' from the Greek word '*pantokratōr*'; and both this Greek word, like the more classical '*pankratēs*', and 'almighty' itself suggest God's having power *over* all things. On the other hand the English word 'omnipotent' would ordinarily be taken to imply ability to *do* everything; the Latin word '*omnipotens*' also predominantly has this meaning in Scholastic writers, even though in origin it is a Latinization of '*pantocratōr*'. So there already is a tendency to distinguish the two words; and in this work I shall make the distinction a strict one. I shall use the word 'almighty' to express God's power over all things, and I shall take 'omnipotence' to mean ability to do everything.

I think we can in a measure understand what God's almightiness implies, and I shall argue that almightiness so understood must be ascribed to God if we are to retain anything like traditional Christian belief in God. The

3

position as regards omnipotence, or as regards the statement 'God can do everything', seems to me to be very different. Of course even 'God can do everything' may be understood simply as a way of magnifying God by contrast with the impotence of man. McTaggart described it as 'a piece of theological etiquette' to call God omnipotent: Thomas Hobbes, out of reverence for his Maker, would rather say that 'omnipotent' is an attribute of honour. But McTaggart and Hobbes would agree that 'God is omnipotent' or 'God can do everything' is not to be treated as a proposition that can figure as premise or conclusion in a serious theological argument. And I too wish to say this. I have no objection to such ways of speaking if they merely express a desire to give the best honour we can to God our Maker, whose Name only is excellent and whose praise is above Heaven and Earth. But theologians have tried *to prove* that God can do everything, or to derive conclusions from this thesis as a premise. I think such attempts have been wholly unsuccessful. When people have tried to read into 'God can do everything' a signification not of Pious Intention but of Philosophical Truth, they have only landed themselves in intractable problems and hopeless confusions; no graspable sense has ever been given to this sentence that did not lead to self-contradiction or at least to conclusions manifestly untenable from the Christian point of view.

I shall return to this; but I must first develop what I have to say about God's almightiness, or power over all things. God is not only more powerful than any creature; no creature can compete with God in power, even unsuccessfully. For God is also the source of all power; any power a creature has comes from God and is maintained only for such time as God wills. Nebuchadnezzar submitted to praise and adore the God of heaven because he was forced by experience to realize that only by God's favour did his wits hold together from one end of a blasphemous sentence to the other end. Nobody can deceive God or circumvent him or frustrate him; and there is no question of God's trying to do anything and failing. In Heaven and on Earth, God does whatever he will. We shall see that some propositions of the form 'God cannot do so-and-so' have to be accepted as true; but what God cannot be said to be able to do he likewise cannot will to do; we cannot drive a logical wedge between his power and his will, which are, as the Scholastics said, really identical, and there is no application to God of the concept of trying but failing.

I shall not spend time on citations of Scripture and tradition to show that this doctrine of God's almightiness is authentically Christian; nor shall I here develop rational grounds for believing it is a true doctrine. But it is quite easy to show that this doctrine is indispensable for Christianity, not a bit of old metaphysical luggage that can be abandoned with relief. For Christianity requires an absolute faith in the promises of God: specifically, faith in the promise that some day the whole human race will be delivered and blessed by the establishment of the Kingdom of God. If God were not almighty, he might will and not do; sincerely promise, but find fulfilment beyond his power. Men might prove untamable and incorrigible, and might kill themselves through war or pollution before God's salvific plan for them could come into force. It is useless to say that after the end of this earthly life men would live again; for as I have argued elsewhere, only the promise of God can give us any confidence that there will be an after-life for men, and if God were not almighty, this promise too might fail. If God is true and just and unchangeable and almighty, we can have absolute confidence in his promises: otherwise we cannot, and there would be an end of Christianity.

A Christian must therefore believe that God is almighty; but he need not believe that God can do everything. Indeed, the very argument I have just used shows that a Christian must not believe that God can do everything: for he may not believe that God could possibly break his own word. Nor can a Christian even believe that God can do everything that is logically possible; for breaking one's word is certainly a logically possible feat.

It seems to me, therefore, that the tangles in which people have enmeshed themselves when trying to give the expression 'God can do everything' an intelligible and acceptable content are tangles that a Christian believer has no need to enmesh himself in; the spectacle of others enmeshed may sadden him, but need not cause him to stumble in the way of faith. The denial that God is omnipotent, or able to do everything, may seem dishonouring to God; but when we see where the contrary affirmation, in its various forms, has led, we may well cry out with Hobbes: 'Can any man think God is served with such absurdities? ... As if it were an acknowledgment of the Divine Power, to say, that which is, is not; or that which has been, has not been.'

I shall consider four main theories of omnipotence. The

first holds that God can do everything absolutely; everything that can be expressed in a string of words that makes sense; even if that sense can be shown to be self-contradictory, God is not bound in action, as we are in thought, by the laws of logic. I shall speak of this as the doctrine that God is *absolutely* omnipotent.

The second doctrine is that a proposition 'God can do so-and-so' is true when and only when 'so-and-so' represents a logically consistent description.

The third doctrine is that 'God *can* do so-and-so' is true just if 'God does so-and-so' is logically consistent. This is a weaker doctrine than the second; for 'God is doing so-and-so' is logically consistent only when 'so-and-so' represents a logically consistent description, but on the other hand there may be consistently describable feats which it would involve contradiction to suppose done *by God*.

The last and weakest view is that the realm of what can be done or brought about includes all logical possibilities for God's future action: that whenever 'God *will* bring so-and-so about' is logically possible, 'God *can* bring so-and-so about' is true.

The first sense of 'omnipotent' in which people have believed God to be omnipotent implies precisely: ability to do absolutely everything, everything describable. You mention it, and God can do it. McTaggart insisted on using 'omnipotent' in this sense only; from an historical point of view we may of course say that he imposed on the word a sense which it, and the corresponding Latin word, have not always borne. But Broad seems to me clearly unjust to McTaggart when he implies that in demolishing this doctrine of omnipotence McTaggart was just knocking down a man of straw. As Broad must surely have known, at least one great philosopher, Descartes, deliberately adopted and defended this doctrine of omnipotence: what I shall call the doctrine of absolute omnipotence.

As Descartes himself remarked, nothing is too absurd for some philosopher to have said it some time; I once read an article about an Indian school of philosophers who were alleged to maintain that it is only a delusion, which the wise can overcome, that anything exists at all; so perhaps it would not matter all that much that a philosopher is found to defend absolute omnipotence. Perhaps it would not matter all that much that the philosopher in question was a very great one; for very great philosophers have maintained the most preposterous theses. What does make the denial of absolute omnipotence important is not that we are thereby denying what a philosopher, a very great philosopher, thought he must assert, but that this doctrine has a live influence on people's religious thought; I should of course say, a pernicious influence. Some naive Christians would explicitly assert the doctrine; and moreover, I think McTaggart was right in believing that in popular religious thought a covert appeal to the doctrine is sometimes made even by people who would deny it if it were explicitly stated to them and its manifest consequences pointed out.

McTaggart may well have come into contact with naive Protestant defenders of absolute omnipotence when he was defending his atheist faith at his public school. The opinion is certainly not dead, as I can testify from personal experience. For many years I used to teach the philosophy of Descartes in a special course for under-graduates reading French; year by year, there were always two or three of them who embraced Descartes' defence of absolute omnipotence *con amore* and protested indignantly when I described the doctrine as incoherent. It would of course have been no good to say I was follow-ing Doctors of the Church in rejecting the doctrine; I did in the end find a way of producing silence, though not, I fear, conviction, and going on to other topics of discus-sion; I cited the passages of the Epistle to the Hebrews which say explicitly that God cannot swear by anything greater than himself (vi.13) or break his word (vi.18). Fortunately none of them ever thought of resorting to the ultimate weapon which, as I believe George Mavrodes remarked, is available to the defender of absolute omni-potence; namely, he can always say: 'Well, you've stated a difficulty, but of course being omnipotent God can over-come that difficulty, though I don't see how.' But what I may call, borrowing from C. S. Lewis's story, victory by the Deplorable Word is a barren one; as barren as a victory by an incessant demand that your adversary should prove his premises or define his terms.

Let us leave these naive defenders in their entrenched position and return for a moment to Descartes. Descartes held that the truths of logic and arithmetic are freely made to be true by God's will. To be sure we clearly and distinctly see that these truths are necessary; they are necessary in our world, and in giving us our mental endowments God gave us the right sort of clear and dis-tinct ideas to see the necessity. But though they are necessary, they are not necessarily necessary; God could have freely chosen to make a different sort of world, in which other things would have been necessary truths. The possibility of such another world is something we cannot *comprehend*, but only dimly *apprehend*; Descartes uses the simile that we may girdle a tree-trunk with our arms but not a mountain – but we can *touch* the mountain. Proper understanding of the possibility would be possessed by God, or, no doubt, by creatures in the alternative world, who would be endowed by God with clear and distinct ideas corresponding to the necessities of their world.

In recent years, unsound philosophies have been defended by what I may call shyster logicians: some of the more dubious recent developments of modal logic could certainly be used to defend Descartes. A system in which 'possibly p' were a theorem, in which everything is possible, has indeed never been taken seriously; but modal logicians have taken seriously systems in which 'possibly possibly p', or again 'it is not necessary that necessarily p', would be a theorem for arbitrary interpretation of 'p'. What is more, some modern modal logicians notoriously take possible worlds very seriously indeed; some of them even go to the length of saying that what you and I vulgarly call the actual world is simply the world we happen to live in. People who take *both* things seriously, both the axiom 'possibly possibly p' and the ontology of possible worlds, would say: You mention any impossibility, and there's a possible world in which that isn't impossible but possible. And this is even further away out than Descartes would wish to go; for he would certainly not wish to say that 'It is possible that God should not exist' is even *possibly* true. So *a fortiori* a shyster logician could fadge up a case for Descartes. But to my mind all that this shows is that modal logic is currently a rather disreputable discipline: not that I think modal notions are inadmissible – on the contrary, I think they are indispensable – but that current professional standards in the discipline are low, and technical ingenuity is mistaken for rigour. On that showing, astrology would be rigorous.

Descartes' motive for believing in absolute omnipotence was not contemptible: it seemed to him that otherwise God would be *subject to* the inexorable laws of logic as Jove was to the decrees of the Fates. The nature of logical truth is a very difficult problem, which I cannot discuss here. The easy conventionalist line, that our arbitrary way of using words is what makes logical truth, seems to me untenable, for reasons that Quine among others has clearly spelled out. If I could follow Quine further in regarding logical laws as natural laws of very great generality; laws revisable in principle, though most unlikely to be revised, in a major theoretical reconstruction; then perhaps after all some rehabilitation of Descartes on this topic might be possible. But in the end I have to say that as we cannot say how a non-logical world would look, we cannot say how a supra-logical God would act or how he could communicate anything to us by way of revelation. So I end as I began: a Christian need not and cannot believe in absolute omnipotence.

It is important that Christians should clearly realize this, because otherwise a half-belief in absolute omnipotence may work in their minds subterraneously. As I said, I think McTaggart was absolutely right in drawing attention to this danger. One and the same man may deny the doctrine of absolute omnipotence when the doctrine is clearly put to him, and yet reassure himself that God can certainly do so-and-so by using *merely* the premise of God's omnipotence. And McTaggart is saying this is indefensible. At the very least this 'so-and-so' must represent a logically consistent description of a feat; and proofs of logical consistency are notoriously not always easy. Nor, as we shall see, are our troubles at an end if we assume that God *can* do anything whose description is logically consistent.

Logical consistency in the description of the feat is certainly a *necessary* condition for the truth of 'God can do so-and-so': if 'so-and-so' represents an inconsistent description of a feat, then 'God can do so-and-so' is certainly a false and impossible proposition, since it entails 'It could be the case that so-and-so came about'; so, by contraposition, if 'God can do so-and-so' is to be true, or even logically possible, then 'so-and-so' must represent a logically consistent description of a feat. And whereas only a minority of Christians have explicitly believed in absolute omnipotence, many have believed that a proposition of the form 'God can do so-and-so' is true whenever 'so-and-so' represents a description of a logically possible feat. This is our second doctrine of omnipotence. One classic statement of this comes in the *Summa Theologica* Ia q. 25 art. 3. Aquinas rightly says that we cannot explain 'God can do everything' in terms of what is within the power of some agent; for 'God can do everything any created agent can do', though true, is not a comprehensive enough account of God's power, which exceeds that of any created agent; and 'God can do everything God can do' runs uselessly in a circle. So he puts forward the view that if the description 'so-and-so' is in itself possible through the relation of the terms involved, that is to say, does not involve contradictories' being true together, then 'God can do so-and-so' is true. Many Christian writers have followed Aquinas in saying this; but it is not a position consistently maintainable. As we shall see, Aquinas did not manage to stick to the position himself.

Before I raise the difficulties against this thesis, I wish to expose a common confusion that often leads people to accept it: the confusion between self-contradiction and gibberish. C. S. Lewis in *The Problem of Pain* says that meaningless combinations of words do not suddenly acquire meaning simply because we prefix to them the two other words 'God can', and Antony Flew has quoted this with just approval. But if we take Lewis's words strictly, his point is utterly trivial, and nothing to our purpose. For gibberish, syntactically incoherent combinations of words, is quite different from self-contradictory sentences or descriptions; the latter certainly have an intelligible place in our language.

It is a common move in logic to argue that a set of A, B, C together yield a contradiction, and that therefore A and B as premises yield as conclusion the contradictory of C; some logicians have puritanical objections to that manoeuvre, but I cannot stop to consider them; I am confident, too, that neither Aquinas nor Lewis would share these objections to *reductio ad absurdum*. If, however, a contradictory formula were gibberish, *reductio ad absurdum* certainly would be an illegitimate procedure, indeed it would be a nonsensical one. So we have to say that when 'so-and-so' represents a self-contradictory description of a feat, 'God can do so-and-so' is likewise self-contradictory, but that being self-contradictory it is *not* gibberish, but merely false.

I am afraid the view of omnipotence presently under consideration owes part of its attractiveness to the idea that then 'God can do so-and-so' would never turn out *false*, so that there would be no genuine counterexamples to 'God can do everything'. Aquinas says, in the passage I just now cited: 'What implies contradiction cannot be a word, for no understanding can conceive it.' Aquinas, writing seven centuries ago, is excusable for not being clear about the difference between self-contradiction and gibberish; we are not excusable if we are not. It is not gibberish to say 'a God can bring it about that in Alcalá there lives a barber who shaves all those and only those living in Alcalá who do not shave themselves'; this is a perfectly well-formed sentence, and not on the face of it self-contradictory; all the same, the supposed feat notoriously is self-contradictory, so this statement of what God can do is not nonsense but false.

One instance of a description of a feat that is really but not overtly self-contradictory has some slight importance in the history of conceptions of omnipotence. It appeared obvious to Spinoza that *God can bring about everything that God can bring about*, and that to deny this would be flatly incompatible with God's omnipotence (*Ethics*

I.17, scholium). In fact the italicized sentence is syntactically ambiguous. 'Everything that God can bring about God can bring about' is one possible reading of the sentence, and this is an obvious, indeed trivial predication about God, which must be true if there is a God at all. But the other way of taking the sentence relates to a supposed feat of *bringing about everything that God can bring about* (that is, *all* of these bringable-about things *together*) and it says that God is capable of *this* feat. This is clearly the way Spinoza wishes us to take the sentence. But taken this way, it is not obvious at all; quite the contrary, it's obviously false. For among the things that are severally possible for God to bring about, there are going to be some pairs that are not *com*possible, pairs which it is logically impossible should both come about; and then it is beyond God's power to bring about such a pair together, let alone, to bring about all the things together which he can bring about severally.

This does not give us a description of a *logically possible* feat which God cannot accomplish. However, there is nothing easier than to mention feats which are logically possible but which God cannot do, if Christianity is true. Lying and promise-breaking are logically possible feats: but Christian faith, as I have said, collapses unless we are assured that God cannot lie and cannot break his promises.

This argument is an *ad hominem* argument addressed to Christians; but there are well-known logical arguments to show that on any view there must be some logically possible feats that are beyond God's power. One good example suffices: making a thing which its maker cannot afterwards destroy. This is certainly a possible feat, a feat that some human beings have performed. Can God perform the feat or not? If he cannot there is already some logically possible feat which God cannot perform. If God can perform the feat, then let us suppose that he does: *ponatur in esse*, as medieval logicians say. Then we are supposing God to have brought about a situation in which he *has* made something he cannot destroy; and in that situation destroying this thing is a *logically* possible feat that God cannot accomplish, for we surely cannot admit the idea of a creature whose destruction is logically *im*possible.

There have been various attempts to meet this argument. The most interesting one is that the proposition 'God cannot make a thing that he cannot destroy' can be turned round to 'Any thing that God can make he can destroy' – and this does not even look like an objection to God's being able to do everything logically possible. But this reply involves the very same bracketing fallacy that I exposed a moment ago in Spinoza. There, you will remember, we had to distinguish two ways of taking 'God can bring about everything that God can bring about':

A. Everything that God can bring about, God can bring about.

B. God can bring about the following feat: to bring about everything that God can bring about.

And we saw that A is trivially true, given that there *is* a God, and B certainly false. Here, similarly, we have to distinguish two senses of 'God cannot make a thing that its maker cannot destroy':

A. Anything that its maker cannot destroy, God cannot make.

B. God cannot bring about the following feat: to make something that its maker cannot destroy.

And here A does contrapose, as the objectors would have it, to 'Anything that God can make, its maker can destroy', which on the face of it says nothing against God's power to do anything logically possible. But just as in the Spinoza example, the B reading purports to describe a single feat, *bringing about everything that God can bring about* (this feat, I argued, is impossible for God, because logically impossible): so in our present case, the B reading purports to describe a single feat, *making something that its maker cannot destroy*. This, as I said, is a logically possible feat, a feat that men sometimes do perform; so we may press the question whether this is a feat God can accomplish or not; and either way there will be some *logically possible* feat God cannot accomplish. So this notion of omnipotence, like the Cartesian idea of absolute omnipotence, turns out to be obviously incompatible with Christian faith, and moreover logically untenable.

Let us see, then, if we fare any better with the third theory: the theory that the only condition for the truth of 'God can do so-and-so' is that 'God does so-and-so' or 'God is doing so-and-so' must be logically possible. As I said, this imposes a more restrictive condition than the second theory: for there are many feats that we can consistently suppose to be performed but cannot consistently suppose to be performed by God. This theory might thus get us out of the logical trouble that arose with the second theory about the feat: *making a thing that its maker cannot destroy*. For though this is a logically possible feat, a feat some creatures do perform, it might well be argued that '*God* has made a thing that its maker cannot destroy' is a proposition with a buried inconsistency in it; and if so, then on the present account of omnipotence we need not say 'God *can* make a thing that its maker cannot destroy'.

This suggestion also, however, can easily be refuted by an example of great philosophical importance that I borrow from Aquinas. 'It comes about that Miss X never loses her virginity' is plainly a logically possible proposition: and so also is 'God brings it about that Miss X never loses her virginity'. All the same, if it so happens that Miss X has already lost her virginity, 'God *can* bring it about that Miss X never loses her virginity' is false (Ia q. 25 art. 4 ad 3 um). Before Miss X had lost her virginity, it would have been true to say this very thing; so what we can truly say about what God can do will be different at different times. This appears to imply a change in God, but Aquinas would certainly say, and I think rightly, that it doesn't really do so. It is just like the case of Socrates coming to be shorter than Theaetetus because Theaetetus grows up; here, the change is on the side of Theaetetus not of Socrates. So in our case, the change is really in Miss X not in God; something about her passes from the realm of possibility to the realm of *fait accompli*, and thus *no longer* comes under the concept of the accomplishable,

deficit a ratione possibilium (Aquinas, *loc. cit.*, ad 2 um).
I think Aquinas's position here is strongly defensible; but
if he does defend it, he has abandoned the position that
God can do everything that it is not *a priori* impossible
for God to do, let alone the position that God can bring
about everything describable in a logically consistent way.

Is it *a priori* impossible for God to do something
wicked? And if not, *could* God do something wicked?
There have been expressed earnest thoughts about this:
I came across them in that favourite of modern moral
philosophers, Richard Price. We must distinguish, he
argues, between God's natural and his moral attributes: if
God is a free moral being, even as we are, it must not be
absolutely impossible for God to do something wicked.
There must be just a chance that God should do something wicked: no doubt it will be a really infinitesimal
chance (after all, God has persevered in ways of virtue
on a vast scale for inconceivably long) but the chance
must be there, or God isn't free and isn't therefore laud-
able for his goodness. The way this reverend gentleman
commends his Maker's morals is so startling that you
may suspect me of misrepresentation; I can only ask any
sceptic to check in Daiches Raphael's edition of Price's
work! Further comment on my part is I hope needless.

A much more restrained version of the same sort of
thing is to be found in the Scholastic distinction between
God's *potentia absoluta* and *potentia ordinata*. (There
are various acceptations of this distinction; I am here con-
sidering only one.) The former is God's power considered
in abstraction from his wisdom and goodness, the latter is
God's power considered as controlled in its exercise by

his wisdom and goodness. Well, as regards a man it makes good sense to say: 'He has the bodily and mental power to do so-and-so, but he certainly will not, it would be pointlessly silly and wicked.' But does anything remotely like this make sense to say about Almighty God? If not, the Scholastic distinction I have cited is wholly frivolous.

Let us consider our fourth try. Could it be said that the 'everything' in 'God can do everything' refers precisely to things that are not in the realm of *fait accompli* but of futurity? This will not do either. If God can promulgate promises to men, then as regards any promises that are not yet fulfilled we know that they certainly will be fulfilled: and in that case God clearly has not a *potentia ad utrumque*, a two-way power, of either actualizing the event that will fulfil the promise or not actualizing it. God can then only do what will fulfil his promise. And if we try to evade this by denying that God can make promises known to men, then we have once more denied something essential to Christian faith, and we are still left with something that God cannot do.

I must here remove the appearance of a fallacy. God cannot but fulfil his promises, I argued; so he has not a two-way power, *potentia ad utrumque*, as regards these particular future events. This argument may have seemed to involve the fallacy made notorious in medieval logical treatises, of confusing the necessity by which something follows (*necessitas consequentiae*) with the necessity of that very thing which follows (*necessitas consequentis*). If it is impossible for God to promise and not perform, then if we know God has promised something we may infer with certainty that he will perform it. Surely, it may be urged, this is enough for Christian faith and hope; we need not go on to say that God *cannot not* bring about the future event in question. If we do that, are we not precisely committing the hoary modal fallacy I have just described?

I answer that there are various senses of 'necessary'. The future occurrence of such-and-such, when God has promised that such-and-such shall be, is of course not logically necessary; but it may be necessary in the sense of being, as Arthur Prior puts it, now unpreventable. If God *has* promised that Israel shall be saved, then there is nothing that anybody, even God, can do about that; this past state of affairs is now unpreventable. But it is also necessary in the same way that if God has promised then he will perform; God cannot do anything about that either – cannot make himself liable to break his word. So we have as premises 'Necessarily p' and 'Necessarily if p then q', in the same sense of 'necessarily'; and from these premises it not merely necessarily follows that q but moreover the conclusion in the necessitated form, 'Necessarily q' with the same sense of 'necessarily', follows from the premises. So if God has promised that Israel shall be saved, the future salvation of Israel is not only certain but inevitable; God must save Israel, because he cannot not save Israel without breaking his word given in the past and he can neither alter the past nor break his word.

Again, in regard to this and other arguments, some people may have felt discomfort at my not drawing in relation to God the sort of distinction between various applications of 'can' that are made in human affairs: the 'can' of knowing how to, the 'can' of physical power to, the 'can' of opportunity, the 'can' of what fits in with one's plans. But of course the way we make these distinct applications of 'he can' to a human agent will not be open if we are talking about God. There is no question of God's knowing how but lacking the strength, or being physically able to but not knowing how; moreover (to make a distinction that comes in a logical example of Aristotle's) though there is a right time when God may bring something about, it is inept to speak of his then having the opportunity to do it. (To develop this distinction: if 'x' stands for a finite agent and 'so-and-so' for an act directly in x's power, there is little difference between 'At time t it is suitable for x to bring so-and-so about' and 'It is suitable for x to bring so-and-so about at time t'; but if 'x' means God, the temporal qualification 'at time t' can attach only to what is brought about; God does not live through successive times and find one more suitable than another.)

These distinct applications of 'can' are distinct only for finite and changeable agents, not for a God whose action is universal and whose mind and character and design are unchangeable. There is thus no ground for fear that in talking about God we may illicitly slip from one sort of 'can' to another. What we say God can do is always in respect of his changeless supreme power.

All the same, we have to assert different propositions at different times in order to say truly what God can do. What is past, as I said, ceases to be alterable even by God; and thus the truth-value of a proposition like 'God

can bring it about that Miss X never loses her virginity'
alters once she has lost it. Similarly, God's promise makes
a difference to what we can thereafter truly say God can
do. It is less obvious in this case that the real change
involved is a change in creatures, not in God, than it was
as regards Miss X's virginity; but a little thought should
show that the promulgation or making known of God's
intention, which is involved in a promise, is precisely a
change in the creatures to whom the promise is made.

Thus all the four theories of omnipotence that I have
considered break down. Only the first overtly flouts logic;
but the other three all involve logical contradictions, or so
it seems; and moreover, all these theories have consequences fatal to the truth of Christian faith. The last
point really ought not to surprise us; for the absolute
confidence a Christian must have in God's revelation and
promises involves, as I said at the outset, both a belief
that God is almighty, in the sense I explained, and a belief
that there are certain describable things that God cannot
do and therefore will not do.

If I were to end the discussion at this point, I should
leave an impression of Aquinas's thought that would be
seriously unfair to him; for although in the passage I
cited Aquinas appears verbally committed to our second
theory of omnipotence, it seems clear that this does not
adequately represent his mind. Indeed, it was from
Aquinas himself and from the *Summa Theologica* that I
borrowed an example which refutes even the weaker
third theory, let alone the second one. Moreover, in the
other Summa (Book II, c. 25) there is an instructive list
of things that *Deus omnipotens* is rightly said not to be

able to do. But the mere occurrence of this list makes me doubt whether Aquinas can be said to believe, in any reasonable interpretation, the thesis that God can do everything. That God is almighty in my sense Aquinas obviously did believe; I am suggesting that here his '*omnipotens*' means 'almighty' rather than 'omnipotent'. Aquinas does not say or even imply that he has given an *exhaustive* list of kinds of case in which 'God can do so-and-so' or 'God can make so-and-so' turns out false; so what he says here does not commit him to 'God can do everything' even in the highly unnatural sense 'God can do everything that is not excluded under one or other of the following heads'.

I shall not explore Aquinas's list item by item, because I have made open or tacit use of his considerations at several points in the foregoing and do not wish to repeat myself. But one batch of items raises a specially serious problem. My attention was drawn to the problem by a contribution that the late Mr Michael Foster made orally during a discussion at the Socratic Club in Oxford. Aquinas tells us that if 'doing so-and-so' implies what he calls passive potentiality, then 'God can do so-and-so' is false. On this ground he excluded all of the following:

God can be a body or something of the sort.
God can be tired or oblivious.
God can be angry or sorrowful.
God can suffer violence or be overcome.
God can undergo corruption.

Foster pointed out that as a Christian Aquinas was committed to asserting the possibility of all these things.

Contra factum non valet ratio; it's no good arguing that God cannot do what God has done, and in the Incarnation God did do all these things Aquinas said God cannot do. The Word that is God *was* made flesh (and the literal meaning of the Polish for this is: The Word became a body!); God the Son *was* tired and did sink into the oblivion of sleep; he *was* angry and sorrowful; he was bound like a thief, beaten, and crucified; and though we believe his Body did not decay, it suffered corruption in the sense of becoming a corpse instead of a living body. Christ in the Apocalypse uses of himself the startling words 'I became a corpse', '*egenomēn nekros*', and the Church has always held that the dead Body of Christ during the *triduum mortis* was adorable with Divine worship for its union to the Divine Nature.

Foster's objection to Aquinas is the opposite kind of objection to the ones I have been raising against the various theories of omnipotence I have discussed. I have been saying that these theories say by implication that God *can* do certain things which Christian belief requires one to say God *cannot* do; Foster is objecting that Aquinas's account says God *cannot* do some things which according to Christian faith God *can* do and has in fact done.

It would take me too far to consider how Aquinas might have answered this objection. It would not of course be outside his intellectual milieu; it is the very sort of objection that a Jew or Moor might have used, accepting Aquinas's account of what God cannot do, in order to argue against the Incarnation. I shall simply mention one feature that Aquinas's reply would have had: it would have had to make essential use of the principle 'as', or in Latin '*secundum quod*'. God did become man, so God can become man and have a human body; but God *as* God cannot be man or have a body.

The logic of these propositions with 'as' in them, reduplicative propositions as they are traditionally called, is a still unsolved problem, although as a matter of history it was a problem raised by Aristotle in the *Prior Analytics*. We must not forget that such propositions occur frequently in ordinary discourse; we use them there with an ill-founded confidence that we know our way around. Jones, we say, is Director of the Gnome Works and Mayor of Middletown; he gets a salary *as* Director and an expense allowance *as* Mayor; he signs one letter *as* Director, another *as* Mayor. We say all this, but how far do we understand the logical relations of what we say? Very little, I fear. One might have expected some light and leading from medieval logicians; the theological importance of reduplicative propositions did in fact lead to their figuring as a topic in medieval logical treatises. But I have not found much that is helpful in such treatments as I have read.

I hope to return to this topic later when I see my way clearer. Meanwhile, even though it has nothing directly to do with almightiness or omnipotence, I shall mention one important logical point that is already to be found in Aristotle. A superficial grammatical illusion may make us think that 'A as P is Q' attaches the predicate 'Q' to a complex subject 'A as P'. But Aristotle insists, to my mind rightly, on the analysis: 'A' subject, 'is, as P, Q' predicate – so that we have not a complex subject-term, but a complex predicate-term; clearly, this predicate entails the simple conjunctive predicate 'is both P and Q' but not conversely. This niggling point of logic has in fact some theological importance. When theologians are talking about Christ as God and Christ as Man, they may take the two phrases to be two logical subjects of predication, if they have failed to see the Aristotelian point; and then they are likely to think or half think that Christ as God is one entity or *Gegenstand* and Christ as Man is another. I am sure some theologians have yielded to this temptation, which puts them on a straight road to the Nestorian heresy.

What Aquinas would have done, I repeat, to meet Foster's objection in the mouth of a Jew or Moor is to distinguish between what we say God can do, *simpliciter*, and what we say God *as God* can do, using the reduplicative form of proposition. Now if we do make such a distinction, we are faced with considerable logical complications, particularly if we accept the Aristotelian point about the reduplicative construction. Let us go back to our friend Jones: there is a logical difference between:

1. Jones as Mayor can attend this committee meeting.
2. Jones can as Mayor attend this committee meeting.

as we may see if we spell the two out a little:

1. Jones as Mayor has the opportunity of attending this committee meeting.
2. Jones has the opportunity of (attending this committee meeting as Mayor).

We can easily see now that 1 and 2 are logically distinct:

for one thing, if Jones is not yet Mayor but has an opportunity of becoming Mayor and *then* attending the committee meeting, 2 would be true and 1 false. And if we
want to talk about what Jones as Mayor *cannot* do, the
complexities pile up; for then we have to consider how
the negation can be inserted at one or other position in a
proposition of one of these forms, and how all the results
are logically related.

All this is logical work to be done if we are to be clear
about the implications of saying that God can or cannot
do so-and-so, or again that God *as God* can or cannot do
so-and-so. It is obvious, without my developing the matter
further, that the logic of all this will not be simple. It's a
far cry from the simple method of bringing our question
'Can God do so-and-so?' under a reassuring principle
'God can do *everything*'. But I hope I have made it
clear that any reassurance we get that way is entirely
spurious.

AN IRRELEVANCE OF OMNIPOTENCE

Unfriendly critics of Christian belief have sometimes argued at once that the doctrine of omnipotence is incoherent, and that Christians must face the challenge how to reconcile God's omnipotence with his goodness, given all the evils there are in the world. Such critics are trying to have their cake and eat it: if the doctrine of omnipotence is incoherent, they are necessarily wasting their time and energy if they discuss the problem of evil in terms of God's alleged omnipotence, and so are any Christian apologists who consent to argue on this footing. For if this incoherent doctrine is in fact an integral part of Christian belief, then that is of itself a sufficient objection to Christianity; and thus any discussion of difficulties Christians may have about evil is a waste of time. The critic in that case is not exactly contradicting himself; but if he is right in one part of his argument, then another part – the part we are likely to find developed at greater length – is on his own showing an entirely futile exercise. If on the other hand Christians are not committed to believing in God's omnipotence, then for them there can be no problem how to reconcile God's omnipotence with something else; and then again any discussion of the problem of evil in terms of omnipotence is a waste of time.

I said in the last chapter that so far as I can see, any

thesis that gives a plausible interpretation of the sentence 'God can do everything' is a thesis involving both inherent logical difficulties and conclusions hard to reconcile with traditional Christian belief. Of course I may be mistaken: the sort of arguments I developed very often turn out to contain subtle fallacies, or again I may have ignored some quite natural way of reading 'God can do everything' that would not be open to my sort of objections. But thus far I see no positive reason to doubt what I then argued; so I feel pretty sure that the doctrine of omnipotence neither has a reasonable and coherent interpretation nor is one that Christians need regard themselves as committed to. My view is, therefore, as at present advised, that the problem of evil is wrongly located when it is put in terms of God's omnipotence, and that both sides ought to realize this.

I am not denying, however, that there is a serious problem of evil. For I agreed also that Christians are committed quite inescapably to the dogma that God is *almighty* – that thus he cannot be thwarted or baffled, and does whatever he will in Heaven and on Earth. Now almightiness gives rise to a problem of evil, and one which cannot be so quickly disposed of. If we are to discuss the problem of evil in a worthwhile way, we had best forget about omnipotence and concentrate on the implications of God's being almighty. I owe this insight to McTaggart (*Some Dogmas of Religion*, §§182–91): it seems to me one of his most important contributions to the philosophy of religion. Btfore I get down to this form of the problem of evil I must try to make clear certain points about God's power and will.

An Irrelevance of Omnipotence

The terms '*potentia absoluta*' and '*potentia ordinata*' are used in various ways by Scholastic writers; I have alluded to one attempt to make a distinction with these terms, and have argued that the distinction is bogus. There is no sense in distinguishing what God simply could do from what he could do wisely and well, since he cannot act except wisely and well. But there is another use of the pair that does mark a genuine distinction: namely, it will be said that e.g. absolutely speaking it is within God's power not to save Israel, this is within his *potentia absoluta*, but *given that he has promised* he cannot leave Israel to perish, it is not within his *potentia ordinata*. The distinction, I say, is a genuine one; but I submit – though I should have Aquinas against me over this – that it has somehow got twisted the wrong way round. What we say God can do *simpliciter* is what God can do in the actual state of affairs: and we thus ought not to say 'God can leave Israel to perish' but only 'God *could*, *would* be able, to leave Israel to perish *if* he had not promised otherwise'. (I shall find it often convenient in the sequel to use the adverb '*simpliciter*' in its Scholastic sense: that sense is not at all recondite – it just means that some predication is true just as it stands, without tacit 'provisos, sub-intents, or saving clauses'. 'God can do so-and-so *simpliciter*' means 'God *can* do so-and-so – period'.)

The line I am taking here is parallel to the line taken by Aquinas, and by Hobbes too, about the voluntariness of acts done out of fear. A man without a pistol at his head *would* will that the bank which employs him should keep its money in the till, but with the pistol at

his head what he *does* will is that the robber should have
the money and not blow out the bank clerk's brains. The
object of actual willing is what actually is chosen in the
concrete present circumstances, not what would be chosen
in hypothetically supposed circumstances. This distinction is sometimes called the distinction of antecedent and
consequent will. It is important on several counts to get
the distinction the right way round, and *not* say that the
surrender of the money is involuntary *simpliciter* and
voluntary only hypothetically, namely *if* you have a pistol
to your head. For one thing, getting this distinction the
right way round serves to quash a tedious sophistry in
discussions of free will. People who say, as I should,
that a man is not free to act in the present if the way
he acts is determined by a set of factors outside his own
control are always told that this is a confusion between
being determined and being compelled. But the objector
is on the contrary himself likely to be confused; coercion
by fear, unless a man is in such a crazy panic, *brevis
furor*, that he cannot even think, leaves a man able to
choose what he shall do, but merely gives him a strong
reason to choose one way; whereas coercion by force
means that the man's choice does not enter into the
story. If a man's choice lies not between surrendering his
employer's money and instant death, but between betray-
ing his country and having some peccadillo exposed, we
may be less inclined to excuse him for yielding to the
threat; that we consider the value of the alternatives
involved shows that we do regard yielding as a morally
appraisable choice and not as simply involuntary.

For our present purpose, this notion of what is willed

simpliciter, actually chosen in the concrete situation, is important because this is the sense of will in which God's will is never thwarted. Men can and do act against God's will in the sense of despising his counsel and breaking his commandments; God's declared counsels and commands are called his will in one sense, distinguished in Scholastic jargon by the label *voluntas signi*. And it is in this sense of will too that we pray that God's will may be done on Earth as it is in Heaven; that is, that men may be obedient to God's command and heedful of his counsels. But whatever happens is something God freely brings about or freely allows some created agent to bring about; the way in which, as I have argued, God must needs fulfil his promises is no exception to this freedom, for God was free to promise or not and had perfect foresight of all possible consequences – he cannot be entrapped by his own promises. Whatever God *would* choose to bring about or to allow in other circumstances, what he *does* bring about or allow is just what he chooses.

If I may now revert to what I said about the power of God, we may observe as I said a parallelism between what God wills *simpliciter* and what God can do *simpliciter*. There is no case in which 'God wills so-and-so', *simpliciter*, is true and 'God can bring about so-and-so', *simpliciter*, is false. God of course can do whatever he does; and he does whatever he will. Even if what happens is due to some finite agent other than God who acts voluntarily, God cannot, so to say, be denied responsibility; for as I said before, the power of the finite agent derives from God originally, and its continuing exercise again depends on God's will.

But now we come to the crux of the matter. McTaggart has questioned whether for an almighty God the distinction between antecedent and consequent will is maintainable, and has argued that a being to whose antecedent will much in this universe were not repugnant would not be perfectly good. This is a serious challenge to traditional theodicies.

McTaggart in fact speaks not of an almighty, but of a creative, God; but it seems clear that he conceived his creative God as being, in my sense, almighty – what God cannot be said to do, he likewise cannot be said to will to do (*Some Dogmas of Religion*, §188). And it seems clear that being almighty and being creative do in fact go together. A God who was not a Creator would be acting within a universe containing other agents whose power did not depend on him, and so would not be almighty. Christians are of course anyhow committed to God's being both.

The distinction between antecedent and consequent will is certainly going to be difficult of application to God. It is customarily illustrated by examples to which there can be nothing parallel in God's case – like the merchantman's captain who throws his wares overboard in a storm: antecedently he wills to bring them into port, consequently upon the storm he wills to throw them overboard. But the captain only does not will rather to allay the storm because this is not open to him; he is not one whom wind and sea obey.

Moreover, the very notion of means and ends is difficult to apply to God. The ordinary notion of means and ends involves that the agent chose the means because he wills the end. But God cannot be said to will or choose anything on account of some cause; as regards what happens in the created world, God's will is the first cause and itself has no cause – otherwise we should get a regress about the causation of God's willing. It is thus that Aquinas (Ia q.19 a.5) says of God '*Non propter hoc vult hoc*' – he does not will one thing on account of another.

Denying that God adopts means in order to secure ends after the fashion of finite agents does not, I think, mean that we need reject the apparent teleology in the world, particularly in the world of living things, as a delusion; I think it is extreme folly to do that, and only fashion can make people account for the ostensible teleology by the idea that of many kinds of things just those survived which chanced to be viable.

But teleology may be something different from an agent's being caused to choose means by his desire of the end. I shall revert to the subject of teleological explanation. For the moment I shall just say briefly that if we are to take final causes seriously, then we must regard the form of explanation 'Why p? p in order that q' as an ultimate form; we must not reduce it to the form 'p because an agent first had the desire that q', where a desire is regarded as one kind of event. This, as has often been said in objection to Aristotle, would reduce a final cause to one particular sort of efficient cause. It seems clear, as a matter of history, that Aristotle did recognize final causes in nature without believing à la Schopenhauer in an unconscious will in things and without believing either in Paley's watchmaker God who craftily

35

adapted means to ends. But the exposition and defence of a teleological explanatory framework would take me far from my present subject.

For the present I return to what Aquinas says of God in the passage I cited: in terse lapidary Latin, '*Vult ergo hoc esse propter hoc, sed non propter hoc vult hoc*'. To spell this out: God wills that there should be a universe in which *hoc est propter hoc* – in which teleological explanations of the form 'it comes to pass that p in order that it should come to pass that q' will work; but God is not *induced* to bring it about that p in order that it may be the case that q, because he desires the latter state of affairs; *non propter hoc vult hoc*. 'God has no ends' was the way Thomas Hobbes put it; God has nothing to gain from creating things, or from our praise of him; God's will is the reason why things other than God are, and itself has no reason. I am not denying that God's will is for the good, or affirming that God has set up some arbitrary standard of goodness; but the Divine Nature stands in no need of any good to be got from creation,

> privata dolore omni, privata periclis,
> ipsa suis pollens opibus, nil indiga nostri.

And Lucretius's reference to the absence of grief and fear from the Divine Nature as well as to its self-sufficiency points up the difficulty of distinguishing God's antecedent and consequent will. If God's will cannot be altered by some good it lacks, or deflected from its course by grief or fear, what room is there for a distinction between antecedent and consequent will in God; between what God *would* will if only ... and what God *does* will? And if God does will, *simpliciter*, such a world as this, how can he be good?

Faced with this difficulty, some men have conceived of God as at least capable of making himself need creatures (C. S. Lewis in *The Problem of Pain* hints at this) and as liable to frustration and disappointment. But I think this is a blind alley, as I have said before. To go this way is to surrender the Christian cause at once; the other way one can go on arguing. I should perhaps here consider the frequent apologetic move of saying that we should consider the character and attributes of God not in terms of abstract theological reasoning but as manifested in the character of Jesus Christ. This may be called a neo-Monophysite heresy: that there is only one character or nature in Christ, and that this is humanly recognizable. Those who maintain this thesis cannot have realized how destructive of Christ's claims it is. For he most certainly did not come to reveal to the Jews a God whom hitherto they had not known and whose character they were now to discover in himself; he was a Jewish Rabbi, teaching within a religion that existed among men before he was born. Whatever he claimed for himself, he certainly did not make the absurd and blasphemous claim that his observable human nature was identical with the Divine Nature; if he had, no pious Jew would have listened to him for a moment; and we must not make the claim on his behalf. Christ as man was amazed and disappointed and angered, and knew grief and pain beyond all men; but we shall get nowhere if we try to find such passions in the Divine Nature.

No: McTaggart's difficulty is a real one. He is right in saying that God's nature in action expresses itself by his will; right in saying that we must not think of limitations on God's power as though they were external obstacles – which is an absurd idea as regards an almighty Creator; right in holding that nothing stops God from doing something except that he does not will it – that God is unable to do only what he is also unable to will. McTaggart does not raise the difficulty I have raised about a theodicy that uses the concept of means and ends, at least he does not do so explicitly; in fact in one place (*Some Dogmas of Religion*, § 181) he seems to consider that this concept *could* be applied to a creative God who was not omnipotent (that is, not what I have called *absolutely* omnipotent). But it would be difficult indeed to defend the application of this concept to a being for whom the distinction of antecedent and consequent will did not exist; perhaps the passage where McTaggart suggests the contrary is only a temporary dialectical concession. Anyhow we have seen that on Aquinas's view the means-and-end concept cannot properly be applied to the Divine will, and his reasons for his view appear sound.

My purpose has been to bring this difficulty sharply before your eyes, not to resolve it. I think a great deal of harm has been done by people thinking the problem of evil needs to be discussed in terms of how omnipotent Omnipotence is. I argued in the last chapter that sense is not to be made of 'God can do everything', and I have argued this time that the real problem lies elsewhere. If I succeeded, as McTaggart unfortunately did not, in shifting the field of debate, I should count that worth while.

I shall end with a couple of remarks which though they do not resolve the problem of evil are I think relevant to it. It is mere impertinence for someone who holds a noncognitive view of our ascribing good and evil to persons or actions to pretend that on his footing there is any problem of evil at all. If my moral code, let us say, is a system of imperatives that I freely choose to promulgate, or if it amounts to saying 'I approve of this and I hope you will too' – then it is merely grotesque to imagine this sort of thing addressed to God. We have here a mirror-image of the error that God *decrees* good and evil arbitrarily. Only of course if it were so, we should have to respect his decrees; and he needn't respect ours.

3

OMNISCIENCE AND THE FUTURE

God is traditionally regarded as both omnipotent and omniscient; he can do anything, and he knows everything. What is meant by 'anything' in 'can do anything' raises intractable logical problems; but the logic of omniscience starts out looking quite straightforward. We get no such question as whether God can bring about what is self-contradictory; for 'God knows that p' holds only if 'p' itself is true, and if it is self-contradictory to say that p, then of course God does not know that p. 'God knows that p' is true if and only if the plain 'p' is true. And whenever it makes sense to ask whether, or who, or why, then we may assert that God knows whether, or who, or why; in ordinary language, of course, such assertions are often a rhetorical way of posing a question when we despair of getting an answer.

We need not lose our heads in dealing with tensed propositions; we need only stick to the simple rule I have just given. In 1939 it was true to say 'Hitler is alive'; it was therefore true to say in 1939 'God knows that Hitler is alive'. In 1970 it was true to say 'Hitler is dead'; it was therefore true to say in 1970 'God knows that Hitler is dead'. At no time was it true to say 'God knows that Hitler is alive and God knows that Hitler is dead'; for otherwise it would at some time have been true to say 'Hitler is alive and Hitler is dead'.

It may be said that allowing such inferences commits us to saying that God's knowledge, and thus his state of mind, was different in 1939 and 1970, so that God would be changeable. But Aquinas would deny that this follows; and I think Aquinas was right. From the time when Plato wrote the *Theaetetus*, it has been notorious that our being able to say different things truly about a thing A at different times does not imply that A itself must have changed, though no doubt *something* must have changed. Socrates is now taller than Theaetetus, now shorter; not because Socrates has changed, but because Theaetetus has grown up; the description we give of Socrates has to be different because of a change in Theaetetus. Similarly, the description we give of God's knowledge concerning Hitler has to be different after Hitler's death; it is manifest that there has been a change on Hitler's side, and that this, in view of the logic of omniscience, makes a difference to what we can truly say about God's knowledge; it is not manifest that there must have been a real change of mind on God's side. And Aquinas can say this even though he explicitly rejects 'Whatever God did know he does know' if the 'whatever' relates to propositions (*enuntiabilia*).

A theologian following Aquinas's way of thinking can get out of check at this move however the game may develop later on; and notice that on the contrary he would be playing into check if he said 'Well, perhaps God's omniscience regarding a changing world means that God is not changeless; that his knowledge has to be changing to keep up to date.' For only an unchanging God can be coherently regarded as causing everything other than himself; it would be merely arbitrary to say that of two mutable beings one required a cause, the other did not. We may dismiss the question 'Who made God?'if we regard God as everlasting and changeless; for only where there is some beginning or some change can there be question of a cause; to dismiss the question if we regard God as changeable is, in Schopenhauer's words, to think you can pay off an argument like a cab when it has taken you as far as you choose to go. Process theology is not a live option.

Some people have not liked the tensed way of speaking about God's knowledge that I am here recommending and have tried to devise ways of speaking more adequate to God's changeless actuality. But we cannot hope in this life for a positive understanding of God's way of knowing things; mortal men who try to speak the tenseless language of the Immortals will find their tongues confounded as at Babel. In particular, it will not do to say that what we see as a series of changes, God sees as an unchanging pattern. For the world God sees is not an unchanging world, and thus if God saw it as unchanging God would be misperceiving it; even if God in seeing the world merely failed to notice the changing aspect of it, he would certainly not be omniscient. The other side of this is that if God rightly saw the world as unchanging, we who see it as changing would be under a delusion. But if time and change are only apparent, not real, features of the world, Christian (or Jewish or Muslim) theism is altogether destroyed. God cannot act in history if there is no history for him to act in, but only a changeless order of things; and the dogma of creation demands an absolute distinction between a changing world and an unchangeable Creator. McTaggart argued that the unreality of time is demonstrable and therefore theism must be false; and I am sure he was right in thinking that you cannot affirm both the unreality of time and the existence of God.

People muddle themselves at this point by saying 'Time is real from our point of view, but not from God's'. This is just a misleading way of saying that the world is seen as temporal by us, but not by God; and then the question has to be pressed: is the world really temporal and changing, or is it not? McTaggart tried hard to form people's intellectual conscience so that they would avoid such woolly phraseology as is often used to burke the question. (It is inexcusable that Ayer should recently by innuendo have ascribed to McTaggart himself the dictum 'Time is real as an appearance'.)

Our only hope of avoiding muddle is to stick to the simple formalities of omniscience, whereby God knows that p if and only if p. This holds good whether the sentence abbreviated to 'p' is tensed or untensed, timeless or past or present or future, necessary or contingent or impossible. For example, 'God knows I am going to be shot tomorrow' is true if and only if I *am* going to be shot tomorrow: and 'God knows $2+2=5$' if and only if $2+2$ is equal to 5 (as of course it is not). Keeping hold of this guideline will not save us from puzzles, but without it we are completely lost and what we say only darkens counsel.

A senseless sentence does not become an intelligible proposition because we write it down after 'God knows

43

that. . .'; and a senseless question does not enable us to make an intelligible statement if we write down its indirect-speech form after 'God knows'. We have to give a sense (say) to the question 'Are there infinitely many twin primes?' before we can intelligently assert 'God knows whether there are infinitely many twin primes'. God's omniscience can never be used to *give* sense to a statement or question. This may seem trivial, but I am pointing out a perennial temptation. I have heard even unbelieving philosophers appeal in argument, not indeed to God's actual omniscience, but to the logical possibility of omniscience, as a way of showing that some expression made good sense. I possess a treatise of formal logic whose author 'justifies' a rule by appealing to the supposed cognitive abilities of Zeus. Such moves are always cheating: either there is already sense and justification without the appeal to Divine knowledge, or else even with this *Deus ex machina* things go wrong. And for our present concern the moral is that before we can hope to talk sense about God's knowledge of the future we must learn to talk sense about the future. Whatever we can say is going to be, we can also say is known by God.

I turn then to what we can and must say in our discourse about the future. The thread of the tangle that I shall lay hold of and hope to get unsnarled is the notion of preventing or avoiding.

What does get prevented? The very posing of the question suggests a wrong answer: an answer in the wrong logical category. The object of the verb 'to prevent' cannot be a name, or a proxy for a name, of an individual entity: if *per impossibile* I could prevent an individual A, A would have to be there to be prevented, and if A were there in the world there would be no prevention of A after all. We may contrast the verbs 'to produce' and 'to destroy'; what is produced is there in the world as the result of the production, what is destroyed is there in the world before it is destroyed, but what is prevented is in Chesterton's phrase absent from the Nature of Things.

We are surprisingly prone to be held captive by one or other picture whereby prevention is doing something *to* what is prevented. Perhaps the picture is that events stand in line waiting to be admitted to the stage of existence, and some of them are refused admission. Or perhaps, that events have a foetal existence in the womb of Time, and some are born, others aborted; such expressions as 'His attempt miscarried' or 'was abortive' express this idea. Let us consider this last picture for a moment; it affords us a ready means of reducing latent nonsense to patent nonsense. Whether a foetus in the womb is a human being or not, certainly it is an identifiable individual, which can be referred to by a proper name chosen *ad hoc*. But if conception is prevented there is no sense in asking which baby it is, or even which embryo it is, that has had its conception prevented. Prevented occurrences can no more be individualized or identified than unconceived babies can.

All this may seem very obvious, and will I trust appear even more obvious when I come on to a true account of prevention. But nonsense may flourish in the darkness of the mind if not exposed, like nasty crawling things under

45

a stone. People sometimes even try to make an honest theory of the individuation of prevented occurrences by using name-variables, say little Es with suffixes, for events that never were and never will be; and just as an attorney may encourage a foolish client to pursue litigation in a hopeless cause, so there are shyster logicians who will encourage theorists by constructing for them what is called free logic. What free logic is intended to be free *from* is the exploded Parmenidean dogma that there is only what there is; an article by a free logician bore the title 'There are things that do not exist'. I fear I read no further than that. Another free logician seriously argued to this effect: since the sentence 'The pilot prevented the worst air disaster of the 1960s' could be true whereas with regard to the same action of the same pilot 'The pilot prevented the assassination of President Johnson' would be false, the air disaster and the assassination must be two different occurrences that didn't occur. We need no elaboration of formal logic to show that this is bunkum. In what class is the accident the pilot prevented supposed to have been the most disastrous member? It is not a member of the class of actual air disasters in the 1960s; and it is surely not meant that what the pilot prevented is the worst air disaster that could possibly have happened in the 1960s. A logic that recognizes such entities as the subject-matter of propositions is no more reputable than would be a logic that recognized the average man as an individual covered by the term 'man'.

What then has ever been prevented? *That* so-and-so occurred. And what is now being prevented by acts that

men take? *That* so-and-so should occur. The right answer
to the question is given, not by a name, but by a
clause; in Latin, which is less fond of abstract nominali-
zations than English, verbs of preventing are regularly
followed by clauses, introduced by a conjunction like
'quominus' or 'quin'. But what then is the so-and-so
whose occurring is prevented? That is a nonsense
question. 'So-and-so occurred' (or 'should occur') functions *as a whole* in the role of a pro-sentence, a proxy
for some actual narrative proposition like 'The aeroplane
crashed into the sea and 100 men were drowned'; it is
nonsense to ask what 'so-and-so' by itself stands for in
this context.

But what then is prevented? Not what did happen, but
assuredly what was going to happen. The aeroplane was
going to crash into the sea and 100 men were going to
be drowned; the pilot's prompt action prevented this. For
not everything that does not happen is prevented: only
what was going to happen. It is this that creates the
absurdity in the schoolboy's essay on 'The Uses of Pins',
which concluded with: 'Finally, pins save millions of
lives every year by not being swallowed'. To save
millions of lives is to prevent its coming about that millions die; and in this case we should not normally say that
millions of people each year were going to die that year,
only keeping off pins in the diet saved them. What we
should normally say is not, in my view, the norm of
truth; but it is because we should not normally *say* that
all these millions were going to die that year that it
sounds absurd to say that keeping off pins in the diet
prevented their death. The example does anyhow bring

47

it out – and I take this to be a truism – that anything that is prevented is something that was going to happen but didn't happen.

But if something did happen, doesn't this show it was after all going to happen? Certainly; but not that it *always* was going to happen. Perhaps, before the preventive action was taken, not this but something else was going to happen; but then the preventive action was taken, and after that *this* was going to happen and did happen. Before the pilot's daring manoeuvre, the plane was going to crash; but after that the plane was going to land safely and she did land safely.

Here it may be in place to lay the ghost of that worst air disaster of the 1960s, which got prevented. Of course it all depends what you mean by 'worst': let us, with some arbitrariness, make number of deaths the criterion. Then for the proposition 'The pilot's prompt action prevented the worst air disaster of the 1960s' to be true, the following must hold good for some number n: first, in no air disaster of the 1960s did as many as n people get killed; secondly, before the pilot's prompt action n people were going to be killed when his plane crashed; thirdly, the pilot's prompt action prevented that the plane should crash and n people be killed. In this analysis there is not even apparent mention of an event that never was, by name or definite description; there are only propositional clauses with the variable 'n' in them, which of course are not names of anything at all and do not even seem to be.

But can anyone ever prevent that what will be, will be? Surprisingly many people are deceived at this point

48

with elementary logical confusions. I do not wish to spend time explaining logical notation; so, at the cost of some prolixity, I shall spell out in the vernacular the differences between the three propositions all confounded together in the ambiguous form of words 'If Jones is going to be hanged, nobody was ever able to prevent Jones's being hanged':

1. Nobody was ever able to prevent its being the case that, if Jones is going to be hanged, then Jones is going to be hanged.
2. It has never been possible that it will be the case both that Jones is hanged and that someone has prevented that Jones should be hanged.
3. If Jones is going to be hanged, then nobody has ever been able to prevent that Jones should be hanged.

When the three propositions are set out like this, it ought to be obvious that they are all different and have different logical structures. (1) and (2), though different, are both trivially true. 'If Jones is going to be hanged, Jones is going to be hanged' is a proposition tautologous in the strictest sense; (1) tells us only that what is stated in such a tautology cannot be prevented from being the case. (2) holds because if something has come about, that *ipso facto* shows that it was not prevented; this is just part of what we mean by 'prevented'. But (3) is different from both (1) and (2), and when we see this we may be little disposed to assent to it.

In fact, (3) is a form of proposition which in practical life we unhesitatingly reject. In a philosopher's study a man may accept the thesis that if something has

49

happened nobody ever was in a position to prevent it; in practical life nobody thinks this way for a moment. Excusing himself for a failure to bring something about, A may say that it was going to happen, thanks to what he did, but that somebody or something else, not under A's control, prevented his plan from being effectual. Or again, A blames B because something happened; B pleads that it was going to happen; A replies 'Of course it was going to happen you idiot! You could see it was going to happen and you could easily have prevented it' (where 'could easily have' = 'were actually in a position to do so with ease'). In the Epistle to the Romans St Paul remarks that in such exchanges, in which men accuse one another or as the case may be excuse themselves, they show their knowledge of the Divine Law written in their hearts: I think this goes for logical laws as well as moral laws. We do know that propositions like (3) are not logically true, and are not always true.

So what was going to happen at an earlier time may not be going to happen at a later time, because of some action taken in the interim. This is the way we can change the future: we can and often do bring it about that it will not be the case that p, although before our action it was going to be the case that p; it was right to say, then, 'It is going to be the case that p'. Before the operation it was right to say 'Johnny is going to bleed to death from the injury': after the operation this was no longer the case.

The mirror-image of this does not hold with regard to the past. If we consider two times t, t′, before something happens, it may be going to happen at t′, the later time, although something incompatible was going to happen at t, the earlier time. The mirror-image of this for past time would read like this, by our switching past and future tenses and 'later' and 'earlier': If we consider two times t, t', *after* something happens, it may have happened at t', the earlier time, although at t, the later time, not this but something incompatible is what has happened. To give a concrete example: At t' Johnny has bled to death from his injury, but by the later time t Johnny did not bleed to death and his injury was quite trivial! Nobody really believes that this is even possible; let alone that human action could bring it about. Agathon the dramatist said even a God could not bring it about: Aristotle, and then Aquinas, rightly quote him with approval. But we can sometimes bring it about that something was going to happen but will not happen: and we all know this. The contrary supposition that whatever is going to happen, always has been going to happen, is not self-contradictory; but we know it is in fact false, so it cannot be logically necessary either.

What we all know about the possibilities of avoidance and prevention makes it seriously misleading to represent time by a single fixed line; with or without a point moving along the line. The picture is not too misleading about the past, for the past cannot be changed; but it is seriously misleading as regards the future, for what is going to happen can sometimes be avoided or prevented.

I am prepared for the objection that I have been systematically equivocating upon two senses of 'going to happen': what actually will happen, and – well, what? What will happen if nothing prevents it, perhaps. My

51

complaint now is not that this phrase just boils down to 'What will happen unless it doesn't'; for I myself do not identify what does not happen with what is prevented. But I do say that the explanation is useless. For what is prevented is always something that is going to happen, in the very sense of 'going to happen' that we are supposed to be explaining; 'prevent' has to be explained in terms of *this* 'going to happen', so we cannot use 'prevent' to explain it. As for the 'actually' in 'what will actually happen', it has no more logical force than a thump on the table has.

When people put up such objections, a picture holds them captive: the picture of a futurity that *is there*, only invisible to us. Other things they think will of course be incompatible with this picture; and they may say I have caricatured them. But if they are captivated by this picture, their false thought will sometimes come to the surface; sometimes very comically. For example, J. J. C. Smart in his preface to an anthology *Problems of Space and Time* (Problems of Philosophy Series; The Macmillan Co., NY, 1964) writes as follows: 'A man can change his trousers, his club, or his job. Perhaps he may even change the course of world history or the state of scientific thought. But one thing he cannot change is the future, since whatever he brings about is the future, and nothing else is, or ever was.' (p. 21) 'Or ever was', indeed! If A is bringing something about, no doubt that is what *is now* going to happen; but what has Smart done to show that it *always was* going to happen, even before A's action? Nothing; he has merely asserted it.

Future-land is a region of fairytale. 'The future' consists of certain actual trends and tendencies in the present that have not yet been fulfilled. What the Moving Finger has once writ cannot be erased: either by tears of repentance, or by the wit of man inventing a time machine, or by the very dubious piety of praying that something may or may not *have* happened (I have written about the last matter elsewhere). But ahead of where the Moving Finger has writ there is only blank paper; no X-ray vision can reveal what is going to stand there, any more than some scientific treatment of the paper on my desk can show what words I am going to inscribe on it.

But surely here I have only set up my own picture of a Moving Finger that writes against the picture of the future as an undiscovered country; and is my picture any more defensible? I imagine what has been written as something permanent and inspectable, what has not yet been written as blank indeterminateness; and this is well enough for actual writing; but if we look at what I am representing in this picture, surely only what is present is actually there, and the past no more available for inspection than the future. The writing we see is a present reality; that it once was written is inferential; and can we not make inferences also about the future?

Here we are in great danger of being trapped, as Parmenides was, by an ambiguity (our 'to be' and Greek '*einai*' share this ambiguity). Parmenides argued that there is only what is; so it must be mere words to speak of past and future. The mistake he made comes out clearly in a riddle that I quote from Plutarch's *Life of Alexander*: 'Are there more men alive or dead?' 'More alive: for the dead are not.' It is true that the dead are not in this sense: if we take 'X' to be any name of a man who is dead, 'X is not', i.e. 'X is no more' or 'X no longer exists', will be true. But it is false that there are no dead men, and on the contrary true that there are a lot of dead men; for there are a lot of names, naming different men, which can be substituted for 'X' in 'X is dead' so as to yield a true proposition. This explanation of the ambiguity presupposes that we can use proper names to refer to dead men, to men who are no more; Parmenides would no doubt have denied this, but I see no reason to accept his view. It is essential to the role of names in language that we can name what is not present in our environment and enunciate propositions about it; a firm grasp of this fact will probably remove the temptation to think that what has ceased to be can no longer be named.

The past, then, though it is not presently actual, does exist in the sense of 'exist' expressed in formal logic by the existential quantifier. We can significantly and truly enunciate propositions '*a F*s', where '*a*' is a proper name of an object that has ceased to exist and '*F*' goes proxy for some verb-phrase; and from '*a F*s' we may infer 'For some *x*, *x F*s' or 'There is an *x* for which we have *x F*s (not, of course, 'There is an *x* such that *x* presently exists and *x F*s').

Now in this sense of 'exists', in which the past does exist, I wish to deny that the future exists. What no longer exists can be named; but you can no more name an as yet non-existent object than you can christen a baby not yet conceived, or a bell not yet cast. You can of course pick a name *for* an as yet non-existent object; but

such a name is not a name *of* an object until it has an
object to name. And so existential quantification cannot
be applied to objects that do not yet exist. One can
indeed say 'There will be a so-and-so'; but this is of the
form 'It will be the case for some x ...', not of the form
'For some x it will be the case that ...' From 'There is
an as yet unactualized potentiality of there being an x
such that x F's' it does not follow even though it may be
true, that there is a (namable) x such that there is an as
yet unactualized potentiality of x's F'ing. There is thus an
ineradicable generality, or lack of specifiability, in certain
statements about the future.

When we rationally prognosticate the future, we do so
from the tendencies of actual agents in the present
situation. Even for inanimate objects, I should argue,
we need to recognize tendencies to bring about certain
happenings in order to describe what actually does
happen. This vein of thought is commonly held, I know,
to have been exhausted, and it is supposed that causal
laws tell us not about tendencies but about what always
does happen. But I notice that the people who talk this
way still speak about one thing interfering with or preventing the effects that another produces; and I have
come across no explanation of this within the conceptual
apparatus of exceptionless causal generalizations. Further,
we certainly need for our prognostications to know the
desires and intentions of beasts and men. What we know
of beasts we know from a remote analogy with man; and
in the first instance we know of men that they will do
what they say they will do, on condition that they
neither lie, change their minds, or are prevented. This

condition, I should argue, is necessarily fulfilled in most cases: lying and change of mind are necessarily the exception, not the rule, nor could the very concept of intention subsist in a world where most intentions were thwarted.

Such prognostications are grossly fallible; but we do not admit error, only ill luck, in our prognosticating, if we say something 'was going to happen' but was prevented by the unexpected interference of some further agent. Could we conceivably do better than this? In one way, yes, conceivably. If there is a God who has everything under his control, then the way he intends things to be is the way they are going to be; and if such a God revealed his intentions to us, we could say 'He is not a man that he should lie or change his mind; as he has promised, so he will perform.' Of course many people do not believe that such prophetical revelation is even conceivable, let alone actual; failing such revelations, the future is only a subject of uncertain prognostication from presently active tendencies and desires and intentions.

There is no question, anyhow, of *seeing* the future: that is, of seeing the actualization of tendencies not yet fulfilled, i.e. seeing where there is nothing to see. Nor do 'coming events cast their shadows before', as the superstitious say: what is as yet only potential cannot affect anything. In a decadent civilization, intellectuals often dabble with such superstition and go prying into the future, trying to *see* it by some occult means or to find somebody who can. Let us have no truck with that: as Bradley said 'If we dally with superstition, if we leave the honourable daylight, the sun has gone back on the dial of humanity.'

Part of what tempts us to think that, given the right trick, we might *see* the future is that we have at the back of our minds, perhaps quite unawares, a theological tradition which taught that God sees the future and can therefore reveal it to others or let others see it. Those who hold this tradition had no good reason why *only* God can see the future. The reverence I bear to the wise and holy men who have expounded this view does not restrain me from flatly rejecting it: *magis amica veritas*. To say that God sees future events as they are in themselves, in their presentness, and not *as* future, is to ascribe to God either misperception or a patently self-contradictory feat. Misperception is involved if God is supposed to perceive what really is future not *as* future but as present; flat self-contradiction, if what God sees is *both* future *and* simultaneously (since in itself it is just as God sees it) also present. The idea that futurity is a delusive way that things appear to us, and the various transparent disguises of this idea, I have already discussed. I am afraid that the very appearance of self-contradiction in specifying this sort of vision was what encouraged the belief that God, but only God, could attain to it.

I am not denying that God is omniscient about the future; I think God knows the future by *controlling* it. God's knowledge of the future is like man's knowledge of his own intentional actions, not like that of an ideal spectator. This too is an old theological idea, and I think it is much more respectable than the idea of God's seeing

57

the future as present. In Anaxagoras already the perfect knowledge *Nous* has of the future is associated with the unfettered control *Nous* has of the cosmos, which *Nous* can affect without being affected. And in the prologue to the IaIIae of *Summa Theologiae* Aquinas says that just this is the way man is in the image of God: man too is the source of his own deeds; has free choice, and power over his own works. 'I said, You are Gods, and all of you children of the Most High.' (It was singularly perverse of Divine-Right authors to apply this verse only to kings.)

If man is a child of God with power over his own works then we must not view the world as

> a Checker-board of nights and days
> Where Destiny with men for pieces plays.

Rather, God and man alike play in the great game. But God is the supreme Grand Master who has everything under his control. Some of the players are consciously helping his plan, others are trying to hinder it; whatever the finite players do, God's plan will be executed; though various lines of God's play will answer to various moves of the finite players. God cannot be surprised or thwarted or cheated or disappointed. God, like some grand master of chess, can carry out his plan even if he has announced it beforehand. 'On that square,' says the Grand Master, 'I will promote my pawn to Queen and deliver checkmate to my adversary': and it is even so. No line of play that finite players may think of can force God to improvise: his knowledge of the game already embraces all the possible variant lines of play, theirs does not.

This is the picture I would put before you to remove

some difficulties against the doctrine that God has unchangeable knowledge of the future. Jonathan Edwards
would object – cf. the Yale edition of his treatise on *The
Freedom of the Will* – that on this view of things God
would be liable to endless frustration and inconvenience,
and constantly needing to alter his plans because of men's
capricious misdeeds. I can only say that Edwards seems
to me the victim of a false imagination. If I were playing
chess against a grand master he could tell me in advance
exactly how he would checkmate me, and do so; it does
not take much faith to believe that God can so manipulate
events as to bring about his great design, announced
through his Prophets and Apostles and his Son, regardless of what may be done by his willing but ignorant
helpers or by his adversaries. I must say, though, that
Edwards seems to me far less wrong than those 'Biblical'
theologians who put up the heathenish view that God
futilely laments the misdeeds of men, and perhaps think
God *had* to let his Son die, as Zeus had to let Sarpedon
die in the Iliad, though this was not his will.

What I have said is certainly incompatible with some
views of predestination, including Edwards's; but I think
these views have to be rejected anyway, for a reason
stated by Aquinas in a quodlibetal question. He is con-
sidering the question whether the same people will go
to Heaven in the actual world as would have gone to
Heaven if Adam had not sinned. He starts from the
premise that who a man is depends on which parents the
man had; this assumes that reincarnation is not possible,
but I have argued elsewhere that there is no good reason to regard it as possible. Now if Adam had not

sinned, even if sin had crept in later on, men might not have been *so* sinful; in particular, therefore, many men who were begotten in polygamy, incest or adultery, might never have been born; and then their descendants would not have been born either. Well, are we to say that all descendants of such intercourse, to the furthest generation, have no hope of Heaven? Such, says Aquinas, is not the mind of the Church. So what we must say is that some people go to Heaven who would not if Adam had not sinned, because they would not have been there to go to Heaven. In fact, given the actual genealogy of Mary, Aquinas has given grounds for what the old carol says: 'Had not that apple/Ever eaten been/Never had Our Lady/Been Heaven's Queen.' It is clear, of course, that as Quine might say the term 'Adam' does not occur essentially in this argument; all along the line people have committed sins they could have avoided, and if those sins had been avoided many human beings would never have existed to go to Heaven.

A tough predestinarian would not necessarily yield. If sufficiently fierce, he *might* say that only people of wholly legitimate descent do go to Heaven. But Edwards would have found Scriptural difficulties about this. What Edwards would say, in fact, is that God arranged circumstances so that all the sinful acts of lust prerequisite to the eventual begetting of the elect should be duly performed. (See *The Freedom of the Will* pp. 249–50) This view may seem grotesque; but I dare not laugh at it contemptuously, for at the next twist of the argument I am hard put to it not to own Jonathan Edwards the better man.

Omniscience and the Future

At this point candour demands that I should mention a most serious objection to what I have been saying. There is no doubt at all that in Scripture and tradition God is regarded as foreknowing and prophetically declaring that a human being A will sin in some specific way: that Judas will betray his Master, and Peter deny him thrice before the cock crows. The definite foreknowledge that I have spoken of thus far is like the Grand Master's knowledge that he will deliver checkmate with a pawn promoted to Queen on QR8, whatever moves his adversary may make: and God knows in this way what he has determined to bring about. But are we then to say that God determined to bring about the betrayal by Judas, the three denials by Peter? Or are we to seek some other account of such foreknowledge?

Jonathan Edwards, as you might expect, does not shrink from the first horn of this dilemma. 'God knew that if he ordered and brought about such-and-such events, such sins would infallibly follow. As for instance, ... that Judas would betray his Lord, and would soon after hang himself, and die impenitent, and be sent to hell for his horrid wickedness.' (*The Freedom of the Will*, pp. 398–9) Edwards does not like the expression 'God is the author of sin', and prefers to say that God has 'permitted, or not hindered sin'; but this concession says more for his heart than his head. If God brings about certain circumstances and knows that given these circumstances certain sins are causally necessary consequences, then God brings about those very sins. This horrible result is fortunately also incredible. For by the same token God is also the responsible author of all human lies; and, as I have said, a lying God's being revealed in an alleged revelation destroys the credibility of that revelation.

What other explanation is there? The idea that God merely sees the future sins as if they were present, and is no more responsible for them than a man in a high tower watching a murder down below, is one that I have already rejected: not because of anything to do with sin, but because I think this phrase, 'seeing the future as if present', embodies a hopeless confusion. If I was right on this point, I need not enter into any tricky discussion of the conditions in which voluntarily not preventing a sin makes an agent responsible for it.

Another explanation that has been offered is that God *is* cause of the act which is sinful, and thus can foreknow it as it will happen, but is not cause of its sinfulness. I must confess that I find this explanation beyond my understanding. According to this view, God is the cause of all actual, positive characteristics in the sinful act, but not of its sinfulness, which is a defect, a negation. But the rule of right reason, by which the act is adjudged defective and sinful, likewise proceeds from God: it is God's Law promulgated to the mind of man. And so the explanation explains nothing, as Hobbes pointed out. 'A man might as well say, that one man maketh a straight line and a crooked, and another maketh their incongruity.' (*Leviathan*, c.46)

Yet another explanation is that we are to God as characters in a novel are to the author, and God is no more responsible for our sins than Dickens for Fagin's; or perhaps rather, though responsible, not blameworthy, any more than Dickens is. I should find it hard to keep a straight face in bringing this out. It is enough to reply that Judas did exist and Fagin didn't, so that the comparison is useless. 'Judas' is really and successfully used as a proper name: 'Fagin' is not the real name of a second-class citizen of the Universe, but only a word Dickens *pretends* to use as a name.

So after apparently reaching some clarification, we are faced with an intractable problem about God's foreknowledge of human sins. It is not, however, that we have run across a plain contradiction; it is just that an account of Divine foreknowledge which appears capable of answering other questions can give no satisfactory answer to this one. But here I would urge upon you a maxim of Descartes: that we should not give up what we do clearly and distinctly understand because of our failure to comprehend what we know in advance must be beyond our comprehension. I am not here appealing to the incomprehensibility of God; our mind, which is *capax Dei*, can understand some things about God clearly and distinctly – for example, what I have called the simple logic of omniscience. What we cannot hope to understand in this life is sin. Sin is the surd or absurd element in the universe. Aquinas has described sin as a falling away from the skill of the Divine wisdom and the ordering of the Divine goodness; but how then can such a thing be, in a world made and sustained and governed by a wise and good God? Yet there, frightfully, it is: *fieri sentio et excrucior*.

To adapt Kant's words, though we cannot understand sin, we can understand its not being understandable; at least not to us who are sinners. A parable will, I hope, convey my meaning. In his professional life a teacher of philosophy often has to present to his pupils thoughts of other philosophers that appear to him not merely false but radically confused; so that no clear, well-formed sentence of the philosopher's own language can convey the thing that was intended by the subjects of his criticism. If he clarifies their thought in his exposition, he is falsifying it by giving it a clarity it did not possess; but if he presents their thought in its native confusion, how is he to get across to his pupils what the confusion is?

It is a desperate resort here to speak of meaningless noises; that is mere abuse, and one cannot argue against meaningless noises. (This form of philosophical abuse is old; in the *Posterior Analytics* Aristotle described the Platonic theory of Forms as bird-whistlings; but Aristotle wanted to persuade Platonists they were wrong, and he did not go and lecture to the birds.) Nor will the opposite extreme of universal charity help: that though philosophers often say what is not so, they never lapse into confusion and unintelligibility. For the variety of philosophers' conceptual schemes makes it certain that *some* accusations of mixing up categories in a nonsensical way must have hit the mark.

So the philosophy teacher has the inescapable task of trying to describe confusions clearly, and convey to his pupils just what the confusions were. This is difficult enough in practice, in concrete cases; what the theory of the matter should be – a theory that could describe what confused thoughts are without itself lapsing into confusion – I have not the faintest idea. And the fact that

A himself is liable to fall into confusion does not make **A** better qualified to describe other people's confusion, but rather worse. It may be that feeling temptations to a confusion is humanly necessary to a proper understanding of it; but it is not necessary to succumb in order to understand. The man of whom perfect understanding of philosophical confusions might be expected is the paragon who, although tempted at all points as we are, is yet without sin.

A parable, and not just a parable: an illustration. For it is part of traditional Christian doctrine that such things as man's propensity to devise radically confused philosophies, no less than his propensity to lechery and murder, are wounds of Original Sin. And falling into a deep confusion of thought *may* be a personal sin – there *are* sins of the intellect; though in this matter of imputing guilt for confusions we must forbear to judge, for we are sinners all. Looking at our inability to understand or adequately describe philosophical confusion does, I suggest, enable us in a measure to comprehend the incomprehensibility of sin, and moreover to see why it is that being a sinner yourself does not help you to understand sin.

We do not, I conclude, know what it would be like to understand sin; to enter into the sinner's confusion and self-deception without misconceiving it or getting involved in confusion and self-deception oneself. So it is no wonder that just here, about God's knowledge of men's sins, we encounter an obstacle to further explanation. The darkness of sin, which is opaque to us, is transparent only to God, to whom the night is as clear as the day.

The possibility of sin, a Christian must say, arises because God has willed that there should be wills other than his with a real say in what happens in the world. This guarantees only the logical possibility of sin; that the possibility is actualized is something, I have argued, beyond the comprehension of sinful men; though we can see why our sinfulness restricts our understanding. And we may believe that God permits sin only because he wills to produce a kind of virtue that stands in internal relation to the sin; virtue that is exercised in opposition to the sin or for the redemption of the sinner, and thus logically could not exist if the sin did not. We may think this price too high to pay; but are we in our sloth and cowardice the best judges? The matter appears otherwise to God's Saints:

> The soldier saints who row on row
> Burn upwards each to his point of bliss,
> Since, the end of life being manifest,
> He has burned his way through the world to this.

4

ANIMAL PAIN

So far I have been concerned with what some people call God's natural, others his non-moral, attributes: almightiness and omniscience. In the remainder of the book I shall consider whether, assuming these attributes, we may still ascribe goodness to God in view of the evils in the world.

Infliction of unnecessary pain is likely to be chosen by modern writers on moral philosophy as *the* example of an obviously wicked act; and correspondingly the presence of pain in the universe is likely to strike many people of our time as the prime objection to belief that the universe was created by a being worthy of being honoured and loved above all things. It appears to me very shallow thinking to find the main difficulty here; as I have said before, the difficulty that presses in upon me like the Egyptian darkness that could be felt is the existence of sin, of wills that set themselves against the will of God. The pains of human beings cannot be discussed adequately without much more consideration of human sin, and in particular of that calamity which is traditionally called Original Sin; the topic of my next chapter. For the present I shall have little to say about human pain.

The pains of the animal world have gone on for a very long time, and there can be no reasonable doubt that sometimes they are very great. In his book *The Problem of Pain* C. S. Lewis seeks to mitigate the problem by two arguments, both of which appear to me clearly fallacious. One argument is that the pains felt by different sentient beings do not add up: neither A nor B feels the pain of the other, nor is there a compound being A *plus* B to feel the pain of both. Only in theodicy would a man think he could get away with saying the number of victims doesn't matter: a man who has tortured a hundred innocent creatures may very well be worse than a man who has only tortured one, even if it were clear that the one had then suffered a little worse pain than any one out of the hundred. If the infliction of suffering on the innocent is supposed to be evidence against the goodness of God but not logically conclusive evidence, then the accumulation of such evidence must progressively diminish the credibility of God's goodness; and it is useless for Lewis to urge that we should treat only the worst pain suffered by any *one* innocent individual as admissible evidence and ignore all other similar evidence. But if on the contrary it is argued that the infliction of *any* unnecessary pain on an innocent creature is positively *incompatible* with God's perfect goodness, then it is enough of a premise for this anti-theistic argument that *some* such infliction occurs; and then Lewis's argument to reduce the *amount* of pain inflicted is simply irrelevant. Either way the defence fails.

Secondly, Lewis doubts whether animals have enough continuity of consciousness to remember, for example, a previous blow from a whip when the whip falls yet again during the same flogging. The lower animals, Lewis

Animal Pain

tells us, may well have 'sentience' without 'consciousness'; and he urges us to accept this distinction, not by
really clarifying it, but by saying 'it has great authority,
and you would be ill-advised to dismiss it out of hand'.
(*The Problem of Pain*, pp. 119–21) I should have thought
that in the philosophy of mind such an appeal to an
unnamed 'great authority' ought to cut very little ice
indeed; as the scholastics would say, *locus ab auctoritate
infirmissimus*. The notion of consciousness to which
Lewis appeals is the one forged by the dialectic of
Descartes; but Descartes thought that even the vaguest
sentience, such as that of a child that has quickened in
the womb, involves consciousness, and for that matter
involves a *res cogitans* to be conscious; and he denied
consciousness to the lower animals only because he also
denied them sentience. Lewis had not given adequate
grounds for his disagreement with Descartes, nor for
saying that animals have sentience but not consciousness
and have no self or soul to be conscious. Lewis's distinction between sentience and consciousness does not seem
to have much in common with the medieval philosophers'
distinction between sentience and rationality; and it is
pretty clearly not based on any psychologists' empirical
study of animal behaviour either.

Lewis's further arguments on this topic strike me as
grotesque. He suggests that the predatory and parasitic
ways of living were introduced into the animal world
not by God but by the Devil, and that the fecundity of
animals whose offspring must mostly fall victims to
predators or hunger or disease is part of the Devil's
scheme to maximize torture. This neo-Manichean story,

even if it were otherwise remotely credible, could of course do nothing to diminish the force of the argument against the goodness of God drawn from the suffering of animals. For on this account, as Lewis would not deny, God gives the Devil his power over the animals on Earth from moment to moment, and did not so to say make them over irrevocably to the Devil, renouncing his own power and right to interfere; nor yet would Lewis deny that God has full knowledge of what the Devil does. People who are repelled from theism by picturing God in the guise of Wells's cruel vivisectionist Dr Moreau will not be reconciled to theism if they are told that they ought rather to regard God as if he were the proprietor of the island where Dr Moreau lives, a proprietor who is fully cognisant of Dr Moreau's occupation and could easily intervene to stop him but chooses not to interfere. This story of the Devil's share in shaping our natural environment is plainly contrary to the Judaeo-Christian idea of God's dealings with his creatures: in Genesis it is God himself who brings about the existence of such an animal world as there is; we find no hint of any change brought about by the Fall of Man, or by the fall of some angel before the creation of Man; and the predation in the world is Scripturally again ascribed to the way God made and sustains things. 'The lions roaring after their prey do seek their meat from God.'

Another blind alley, in my opinion, is the idea that God willed to produce a varied fauna and flora in our world through evolution by natural selection; as if this global strategy somehow let God off responsibility for the pain individual sentient beings may incidentally have

70

suffered in the course of evolution. Only by gross anthro-
pomorphism can we compare God to an army com-
mander or big business executive, who is responsible for
the main line of policy and not for the details of its
execution. In any event, if there is a God, then the
teleological structure of organisms is ascribable to God;
and I shall argue that the *prima facie* teleological structure of the organic world has not been shown not to be
really teleological by Darwin's speculations. But part of
this teleology is what makes predators and parasites
efficient. If this argument succeeds, the evolutionary
theodicy fails.

I spoke briefly of teleology and teleological explanation
in chapter 2. I now return to the topic. I cannot profess
to have a rounded, finished account of the matter; but I
hope I have discerned some truths and seen through some
fallacies. First, then, to repeat: If we are to recognize
explanation by a final cause as genuinely distinct from
explanation by an efficient cause, then we must reject the
analysis of '*p* in order that *q*' into '*p* because of an
antecedent plan or desire that *q*', where a plan or desire
is regarded as some event that occurs in the mind before
it comes about that *p*. On the contrary: the notions of
desire and of the voluntary themselves need to be explained in terms of the more general notion of teleology,
whose natural linguistic expression is what grammarians
call a final clause; otherwise final causality just becomes
one variety of efficient causality. And when we turn, as
I shall in a later volume of these lectures, to the notion of
voluntariness and freedom, I hope to establish that
something's coming about by a person A's will does not

consist – does not *ever* consist – in the occurrence of some previous motion in a metaphysical part of A called the Will, which motion is then the efficient cause of what is said to be voluntarily done.

This ought to make it easier to grasp the next point: that there need be no incompatibility between final and efficient explanation; there may even be reciprocal explanations, running opposite ways in the two orders. The truth of 'It comes about that *p* because it has previously come about that *q*' nowise excludes the truth of 'It came to pass earlier that *q* in order that it might later be the case that *p*'. So the idea that scientific progress in finding out efficient causes somehow discredits teleological descriptions, or progressively reduces the area of their application, seems to be logically unfounded. I suspect it is influential just because of a vague impression that teleological propositions affirm a rival account of efficient causality which is now shown to be false or superfluous. And this idea of a clash is one for which the commonplace of scholasticism is a sufficient answer: that we can have cases of reciprocal causality, *causae ad invicem*, so long as these are cases where we consider now one, now another, order of causality, *causae in diverso genere*.

I do not wish to imply that Aristotelian philosophy had all the answers: apart from errors of detail (and there were many) about the natural world, it was vitiated, both in Aristotle and in his medieval followers, by a serious confusion. The word for 'end' in Latin and Greek, as in English, makes possible a confusion between the final stage of a process and the point of a process; and an

72

unbalanced diet of examples made matters steadily worse. Aristotle ought to have remembered his own theory of the uniform celestial motions, which he certainly did not regard either as pointless, or as tending towards some final state of rest in an optimum position of the heavenly bodies. (I am afraid some of the medievals disimproved Aristotle's view in just this way: but not they alone – compare Tennyson's 'one far-off divine event to which the whole creation moves', or Teilhard's Omega.) Anyhow we need only consider such examples as the arts of song and dance rather than of architecture to see that the final state need not be the point of the whole activity. I am sure that much discussion about the end of man's life, or of particular human activities, has been vitiated by this fallacy. It is likely to impede clear thought about the teleology of vital processes. Suppose we say that the mayfly grub exists in order that the perfect insect may exist and the perfect insect exists – since it cannot eat, but only reproduce – in order that another lot of grubs may exist: if now we imagine teleology in terms of a temporally final achievement, the whole business may appear futile like the labours of Sisyphus. But that is not the way we ought to think.

Next, let me re-emphasize that to say 'Acorns exist in order that oak-trees may exist' is not to say that God wants oak-trees to grow and sees to it that there are acorns to this end, and is consequently frustrated continually when acorns fail to produce oak-trees. This is a foolish way of thinking, and the folly is aggravated when people speak of such reproductive methods as wasteful. God cannot be wasteful, for he has no resources that he needs to conserve; God does not *need* to produce oak-trees by the elaborate reproductive process by which they are produced; he could produce as many as he wished of oak-trees, or children of Abraham for that matter, 'easily, by the thought of his mind' as Xenophanes said; and he does not *need* to produce oak-trees – he has no needs. God has willed to produce a world in which teleological schemes of explanation work; but the reason for producing the world is his mere free choice, which has no cause.

But explanation by free choice ought to satisfy us in a way that explanation of the form 'That's how things *always* happen' does not. The degree to which the superstition that regularity is self-explanatory prevails is quite astonishing; I remember a colleague who thought it *obvious* that atoms trickling into existence one by one out of nothing at a statistically regular rate was more intelligible than one Big Bang. There is a story I heard – and its authenticity of course does not matter – of how a Russian Tsar sought an explanation of why a soldier stood always on guard in the middle of a certain lawn in the palace grounds. The explanation that it had always been that way, that there was a standing order for this, did not satisfy him; eventually he discovered that a Tsaritsa had put a man on guard to prevent a snowdrop from being trampled down, and the order had never been countermanded. The Tsaritsa's capricious will was a satisfying explanation, beyond which he need not look. Of course people will now say that there are known regularities in terms of which the caprices of Tsaritsas can be explained and predicted 'in principle': and of course this is mere bluff, for no such thing is remotely possible, nor do sensible people seek such regularities.

The description of the living world in teleological terms is so natural that those who deliberately reject it again and again fall back into it. There is a popular belief that Darwin has shown once for all that such teleological detail is all a delusive appearance: it can all be explained by natural selection. I must first rule out of court a gross *ignoratio elenchi*. People who throw doubt on the theory that natural selection suffices to explain the origin of the species we actually find, and to explain away ostensible details of teleology, are often represented as denying that new species evolved by natural descent from previously existing species. This is simply a muddle or a debating trick, on which I shall waste no more words.

Darwin's method in *The Origin of Species* is to put up a challenge of this form: You mention some ostensibly teleological feature of living things, and I will show how it could have arisen through casual variations and the elimination of ill-adapted varieties. And he seems to suppose that the accumulation of many such stories increases the probability of each story. The opposite is the truth. Any one such story is pretty improbable on the face of it; we often have no evidence whatever that such random variation and the perishing of unfit varieties took place as Darwin hypothesizes; and in view of the imperfections of the geological record, the irrecoverable perishing of soft tissues, and the like, we can in many instances be pretty certain that no better evidence is going to be available. The improbability of the whole theory is increased, not diminished, as one unlikely story suceeds another.

This, I shall be told, is a vicious appeal to ignorance: I am urging that we should reject a story as false because there is no conclusive proof that it is true. But this rejoinder misconceives where the burden of proof lies. Someone who wishes us to reject as delusive the *prima facies* of detailed teleology in the living world had better provide himself with pretty good proofs; and it is just too bad for him if he has to say that of course the decisive evidence is irretrievably lost. A man turns up in a lawyer's office claiming to be the lost heir to a baronetcy; his memory is very defective for his alleged early life, and he is fluent in Polish but can speak little English; the documentary proof of his identity, he tells us, was unfortunately destroyed in the bombing of Warsaw, and his memory-gaps are due to a stay in the Oświęcim concentration-camp. Well – it might be so; but he cannot accuse the lawyers of a vicious appeal to ignorance if they refuse to be convinced easily, precisely because of this loss of evidence. And a collection of *several* stories of this sort is *less* likely to be true than any *one* story.

What is more, the ostensibly teleological structures and processes by which animals and plants live include complex reproductive processes which give a strong impression of teleology. Now in order that there should be an origin of *species* by evolution at all, rather than the production of an Empedoclean chaos of monsters, it is necessary that these offspring should have, in each successive generation, a considerable, though not complete, resemblance to their parents, including a resemblance in manner of reproduction. Otherwise a method of reproduction evolved by chance variation would serve for the survival only of *that* generation, not of subsequent ones. The reproductive mechanisms certainly cannot be explained just by saying that creatures which failed to develop them failed to reproduce their kind and perished: without these mechanisms there would be no raw material for any cause of evolution to work upon. So in this case there can be no story of natural selection to replace the ostensible teleological account; why then need we think some such story must account for other ostensibly teleological structures and activities of living things?

In arguing to this conclusion, I have not been trying to ease the task of theodicy: quite the contrary. For among the most striking cases of ostensible teleology are the ways that predators are adapted to catch their prey and the way that parasitic animals like the liver-fluke live and reproduce their kind. By what I am arguing, this teleology should be accepted as genuine. The spectacle of the living world, to an uncaptive mind, is a manifestation of great power and of great wisdom, for which no detail is too small; but there is no evidence or hint that the whole show is organized to minimize pain; nor, for that matter, is there any evidence that pain as such is elaborately contrived, as by Lewis's Devil. The Creator's mind, as manifested in the living world, seems to be characterized by mere indifference to the pain that the elaborate interlocking teleologies of life involve. And with this the nightmare of Dr Moreau seems to return:

particularly since Dr Moreau is represented not as enjoying torment but as fulfilling himself intellectually regardless of the pain he causes.

At this point I make a change of subject. Ought we to expect God the Creator of the world to have virtues like those of men? And ought we to admire and love him above all things even if he has not the character that would be deemed morally good in man? I shall argue that many human virtues cannot possibly be ascribed to God, and that all the same there can be nothing more worthy of love and admiration than God is.

There are certain human virtues that must be ascribed to God in a way befitting his kind of life: God is provident and wise and truthful and faithful to his promises. One cannot think of an illogical world, nor therefore of a world made by an improvident or foolish God; and only a revelation according to which God is truthful and faithful to his promises can begin to be credible. But there are many virtues that it would be obviously absurd to ascribe to God: chastity, courage, honesty, gratitude. Even justice raises severe problems. Commutative justice is out of the question: what can God be given so that he owes something in return? Distributive justice seems very difficult too: since all that a creature has and is is God's gift, how can the question be raised whether God treats equals unequally or not, or whether the differences he has regard to are relevant or irrelevant ones? We may, I believe, ascribe to God retributive justice: reward and punishment; but his rewards and punishments are not arbitrarily annexed by positive law to human deeds.

78

These considerations are pretty straightforward, but are liable then to provoke the reaction that if God is not like a virtuous man then we ought not to admire and love him, or at least not as much as we admire and love virtuous men. But the reaction is perverse. What is being asked is that God should be admired and loved for his great glory, for being God, for being utterly unlike man in nature. (I do not say that Christians never have made an object of worship tha*t was* like a man, indeed like a vicious man; when I read Jonathan Edwards at his worst, I cannot but agree with the words of the Chevalier Ramsay as quoted by Hume: 'The grosser pagans contented themselves with divinizing lust, incest, and adultery, but the predestinarian doctors have divinized cruelty, wrath, fury, vengeance and all the blackest vices.')

God is to be loved and admired above all things because he is all truth and all beauty: the truth and beauty that in the universe is scattered in separate pages, to use Dante's figure, is in God bound up orderly into one volume. And we love truth and beauty by our nature, in so far as our vices and follies do not prevent us. So it is only vice and folly that stop us from loving God above all things. The protest that we ought not so to love and admire him if he does not share the moral perfections proper to his creatures is a mere impertinence.

One virtue, if I am right, that God cannot share with his creatures is the virtue of sympathy with physical suffering. It is virtuous that a man should in measure sympathize with the sufferings of the lower animals:

only in measure, for someone who tried to sympathize with a shark or octopus or herring would be erring by excess as Dr Moreau erred by defect; their life is too alien to ours for sympathy to be anything but folly or affectation. I once heard of a moral philosopher who worried, as he attacked his lamb chop, whether we ought not to avoid unnecessary suffering to animals by turning vegetarian; but then he reflected on all the slugs and bugs that would have to be killed in order to feed the human population; then if we reckon how many slugs and bugs add up, in the way of pain, to one lamb – and so he attacked his lamb chop with renewed zest. And I have never heard the conservationists protest against our genocidal war with the rat, a war prosecuted quite ruthlessly and with means that may cause extreme pain. Let us clear our minds of cant. Sympathy with the pains of animals whose nature we share is, I repeat, a virtue in men, so long as the Aristotelian mean is observed. But it is not a virtue that can reasonably be ascribed to the Divine Nature. God is not an animal as men are, and if he does not change his designs to avoid pain and suffering to animals he is not violating any natural sympathies as Dr Moreau did. Only anthropomorphic imagination allows us to accuse God of cruelty in this regard.

It is not hard to answer the sophistical objection that being men we 'can only judge God by human standards'. The last phrase is merely equivocal. If what is meant is that we men can only judge God by standards that we men judge by, then we have an uninteresting tautology. If what is meant is that our standards for deciding whether God is lovable and admirable must be the same as our standards for deciding whether men are lovable and admirable, then I simply deny this: they need not be and they should not be the same. And if what is meant is that our standards must be standards that men have invented for themselves, then again I reply that they need not be: if Christian faith is true, the spiritual man is more and more taught of God to judge by God's standards, and will in God's good time judge both men and angels. But in saying this I do not wish to conceal how weak that new man is in me, how strong the old man, my worst enemy, whom I see daily in the mirror when I shave.

I wish in conclusion to say something about words of my own that have given scandal. In *God and the Soul* I justified submission to Almighty God simply and solely because he is the Supreme Power, and accepted the charge that this is pure power-worship. This made a bad impression that was not erased by my immediately following words about the Supreme Power's being one that earthly powers do not compete with, even unsuccessfully. All the Divine attributes, if thought out, coincide; God's power and will and knowledge and truth are all one; for, as I argued before, God's knowledge of the world is to be compared not to our speculative knowledge but to our knowledge of our own deeds before we do them; and all Truth is in him, in that his ideas, like an artist's designs, are the measure and cause of what happens in the world; not because his thoughts reflect what happens. God is supreme Power because he is all Truth: great is Truth and strong above all things. To

worship the Supreme Power is to worship the Mind that
invented us and made us real just by thinking of us.
Plainly this attitude, really assented to, is, as I said
before, nothing like cringing before an earthly potentate:
rather, it excludes such cringing. Our knowledge that
God reigns and no detail escapes his Providence may
screw up our courage to the sticking-point where we are
tempted to disobey his Law because of foreseen consequences.

It is no good to plead against our Maker that we
decided to break his Law because, as we saw things, that
was acting for the best. The calculation of a best alternative is anyhow nonsensical, as Arthur Prior showed
in his paper on 'The Consequences of Actions'.[1] It is
further refuted by the thoughts that God will certainly
win the game and my actions cannot stop or hinder
that, so that calculation of a good future for the world
is anyhow God's business, not mine; and that God cannot
be fooled or thwarted, so that I cannot by stealth in his
despite win advantages for myself or those I love by acts
that he has forbidden. There is nothing for it but to
submit and obey.

In writing of the duty of submission to God, Thomas
Hobbes cited the words of Christ to St Paul: It is hard
for thee to kick against the goad. Hard, but not impossible, for men are foolish and obstinate. I have never much
liked the phrase 'the ground of being', but it suggests a
useful picture. 'If you fall on the hard ground and hurt
yourself,' one might say to a fractious child, 'it is no good

[1] Prior, *Papers in Logic and Ethics*, Duckworth, 1976.

getting angry and kicking the ground; you'll hurt your-self more, and you cannot damage the ground; and if you want to get anywhere you can only walk on the ground and not fly through the air. The hardness of the ground that hurts you is the only thing that enables you to walk securely; and the ground will still be there for you to pursue your journey upon, when you come to your senses.'

5

ORIGINAL SIN

Imagine an altar-piece; a triptych, with a centre-piece and two folding leaves. One side depicts Eve yielding to temptation, and thereby entailing upon her posterity the damnable inheritance of sin, misery and death. The other side depicts the angelic salutation to Mary, whose words of humble and obedient acceptance of God's will were the first unsaying of the evil spell that had been cast upon man. In the middle is Christ in glory; his body, though the wounds of love are visible upon it, is now radiant with undying life; he is triumphant over death and sin, the Lord and the destined Judge of all the world. Now imagine that the Eve panel has been stolen or destroyed: the balance and artistic worth of the picture is irreparably spoiled.

This is a feeble comparison for the damage that has been done to the Christian view of the world by rejecting – rethinking, to use a politer word – the doctrine of the Fall of Man. It is often said that in our world and time the Christian story is irrelevant. A curious adjective, when the grimmest Christian prophecies of the last days might seem, even by human calculation, all too likely to be literally fulfilled. But it is easy to see what people mean when they say this. What they have in mind is not full-strength but denatured Christian doctrine. The world at large accepts a very different story from the Christian story: the epic of man's evolution and progress, such as you find in H. G. Wells's *Outline of History* or a hundred other books. What I call denatured Christian doctrine is an attempt to accept this story and yet retain what are taken to be the essentials of Christian doctrine. This attempt, I shall argue, is foredoomed to failure.

In the first place, what reason could anybody have for believing the new Christian story? Why should we be believers in it rather than incredulous? If a remarkable tradition has been continuously preserved through many centuries, continuously from the time when this body of belief first arose, this of course does not exclude its having been from the first a fantastic delusion. But if a tradition really is continuous – and I maintain history shows that this is true of Christian tradition in some of its most important traits, in spite of the lamentable divisions of Christendom – then we are believing what was believed by the founders of the tradition, and we are right in believing it if they were right. Like the gold and cedar of the Ark, truth does not grow old. The founders of the tradition claimed to have their teaching from the lips of the Son of God and from the Holy Spirit that had been given them.

Do we accept this claim or do we not? If we accept it, there is an end of the matter; we must hang on to that truth, though one claiming the authority of an apostle, or an angel, should teach us otherwise. And if we reject it as unfounded, then by all means let us follow this way of the world and try to determine for ourselves how the world came to be and what man's place in it is; but it is mere impertinence for somebody now to set up a claim that he can teach a revised Christian doctrine, superior in important ways to the old doctrine. He cannot establish the truth of his claim by reason, as the world pretends to establish the truth of the epic of evolution and progress. Can he then establish that he has some God-given authority? I do not see how he can. 'Jesus I know, and Paul I know, but who are you?' we may say to him when he sets up as a teacher. Assuredly he cannot say to a sick man 'Get up and walk' (nor is he likely to be able to say 'Silver and gold have I none', either!) and he will be entirely unable to show any sign that he is inspired by the Holy Spirit. His teaching will be a matter of learned conjectures intermixed with such fragments, few or many, of the old tradition as he chooses still to believe. He may choose to believe all this; but he will scarcely persuade a rational outsider, and he can claim no authority that should bind the conscience of a Christian.

I can expect a protest from Roman Catholics and others that tradition is not a dead static thing but a growing thing. Indeed tradition can grow. Many of us have played the party game of Russian Scandals; and the game is not all that different from the scandal-mongering of real life. Of course a human tradition can grow and develop like that. But then there is no reason to believe such a tradition. The claim that such a mutable tradition is to be accepted on authority by each successive generation in the form that it has currently thus assumed is sheer effrontery. The Roman Catholic Church has itself authoritatively repudiated, in the acts of the First Vatican Council, the claim that with the progress of knowledge a doctrine hitherto continuously taught in one sense now needs to be construed in another sense. It is not now my purpose to argue whether the Roman Church or some other Christian denomination can claim to have preserved an unchanged deposit of doctrine. What I am arguing is that only if such a claim is made is the Christian message credible at all.

Truth, I repeat, does not perish and does not change. If it was true 1900 years ago to say that man was made upright in will, and immune, if he remained in that uprightness, from misery and death, but that by his own misdeed man fell from that blessed state, then this cannot have ceased to be true by lapse of time.

Nor can it be said, as could perhaps be said of some ancient ideas, that the conceptual apparatus in which this doctrine is framed is no longer intelligible to us; whatever difficulties there may be in believing the doctrine, it is not too difficult to understand. Moreover, if true, this is clearly an important truth; if false, a most harmful error. It is a matter of history that for 1800 years, despite the division of Christendom, this doctrine counted as what C. S. Lewis called 'mere Christianity'. If Christian tradition could be in error about this, then either it has been irretrievably corrupted in transmission or it was gravely wrong from the first. In the latter case we certainly cannot be Christians: if what was taught in the first century as Divine revelation was in large measure false. Things are not much better in the other case: if there once was a Divine revelation, but it was early corrupted in a substantial way. For how could we then reconstruct the content of the original revelation?

And without such reconstruction we should be almost as ill-informed of the truth about God and man as if no revelation had been given at all.

That is my first thesis: that if the doctrines of the Fall and Original Sin are rejected, then this involves such a sceptical attitude towards Christianity that we can have no possible reason to be Christians. I have thus far not appealed to the special content of the doctrine: I have merely argued that it is both important and (at least in part) intelligible.

Only in part intelligible: Original Sin is a *mystery* of iniquity. Being sinners in a world of sinners, we know it as a fact of experience that a man may have, as we say, every advantage, and perversely throw it all away. That this happens we know; faced with such a disaster, we in vain ask why it had to happen. Sin of its nature is the something we are unable to make fully intelligible to ourselves; all the less able because we ourselves are involved in it.

The doctrine of Original Sin is all the more para-doxical because it is only the *original* sin that infects later human generations. The Law and the Prophets declare the personal responsibility of each man; Ezekiel in par-ticular teaches with much insistence that a good son is not answerable for the wicked deeds of his father, of which his own life has been one long repudiation.

As for what is called collective responsibility – the idea that a man is responsible for the evil done in his environment merely by the act of living in it – I could say much about how much harm this idea has done, but will here say briefly that it is equally repugnant to reason and to Christian teaching. It is the constant teaching of Christ and His Apostles in the New Testament that Christians are to live in the world, but not of it, unspotted by it, like sheep among wolves; if a sheep inevitably became wolfish by the mere fact of living among wolves, these commands and counsels would be idle breath. And only an individual man can have moral responsibility, reason should teach us; just as only an individual man has a mind and will.

By legal fiction, into the nature of which I cannot enter here, a corporation is treated as a person that can commit civil and criminal wrongs; but this is as much a fiction as that whereby under the old Indian Empire a mythical Hindu god used to be recognized as the owner of some property, and therefore capable by his representative of being party to suits in the courts of law. Really, as a lawyer brutally put it, a corporation has neither a soul to be damned nor a body to be kicked. Let us clear our minds of cant and recognize this. And what must be denied to the legal corporation must still more be denied to 'the community'; that is, the casual aggregate of persons that a given individual has to do with in the course of his life: he does not bear their sins, nor they his; not, that is, by merely being around in the same environment, but only by some specifiable acts or omissions of the sort whereby one individual may share the guilt of another's act: defending the wrong done, guilty silence, or the like.

The traditional doctrine is that since the sin of our first parents, men have been conceived and born different in nature from what they would have been had our first parents stood firm under trial. As C. S. Lewis puts it, a new species, not made by God, sinned itself into existence. This is certainly a difficult notion, and I shall return to its difficulties later. What I now wish to suggest is a way that this notion, if we accept it, can explain how children born thereafter are involved in sin; in a wrong direction of the will. Sin is a matter of the will: if Original Sin is not, in Adam's posterity, a matter of the will, then it is not properly sin. But I think we can see how Original Sin in Adam's posterity *is* sin, though it is not sin like the deliberate choice of wrong actions.

Will is not simply, and not primitively, a matter of choice. There is, presupposed to all choosing, a movement of the will towards some things that are wanted naturally; to live, to think, and the like, in short to be a man. If man were as he ought to be, there would be nothing wrong with this natural willing, *voluntas ut natura* as the scholastics called it. But if the nature a man has inherited is flawed, then a will that acquiesces in this flawed nature is perverse from the start; and from this perverse start actual wrong choices will certainly proceed, given time. The misery resulting from wrongdoing cannot destroy the deep-rooted wanting to be what man, by his present nature, is; man cannot so learn by experience that his perverse will cures itself. As the great philosopher Schopenhauer kept saying, *velle non discitur* (willing isn't learned). Nor can suicide, self-destruction, count as a turning of the perverse will in the right direction. Here too Schopenhauer is in the right of the question: he compares the suicide to a man undergoing a painful operation who runs away and embraces the old disease rather than the pain; Schopenhauer regards suicide as the supreme assertion of the perverse will rather than its rejection.

I have found it instructive to read Schopenhauer's writings. The Christianity of his milieu, which he scornfully rejected, was deeply corrupted with worldliness and false optimism, and he could in part see that this was not genuine Christianity but a counterfeit. But he remained to the end of his days irreconcilably anti-Christian. All the same, he seems to me to have been a prophet to his people, like Balaam; like Balaam, too, he longed ineffectually for the peace that he could see came for the righteous; but that was not for him: vanity, ambition, combativeness, a host of human failings denied it to him, and he knew all too well that this was so.

What's wrong with the world, and what is the remedy? Oriental religions answer: sorrow, or ignorance, is what is wrong with the world; enlightenment is the remedy. Schopenhauer fancied himself to be teaching Hindu or Buddhist truth against Christianity; but on his capital point his answers were Christian, not Hindu or Buddhist. What's wrong with the world is sin, or evil will; an evil so radical that it is inborn. And the only remedy for sin is conversion of the will: its turning *against* what comes about by ordinary psychological causes; indeed, Schopenhauer thought it impossible to give a positive conceptual account of how conversion did come about. That it did come about, the lives of holy men and women showed; from our painful and needy condition, we look towards them with helpless longing. Compared with this peace all other aims are

vain dreams, and the great world itself, with all its
stars and galaxies, is nothing.

My account of Schopenhauer is of course one-sided:
there is much in him that is fantastic, much that is
repulsive. But an informed Christian reader can learn
much from him and be strengthened in his faith. Much
of the aversion to Schopenhauer has come from his all
too faithful portrayal of what is evil in man; just as the
bald description of human wickedness, without rhetorical abuse and without palliation, in the historical books
of the Old Testament is unbearably repellent to many
minds. The remedy he understood only negatively and
externally. But he stands there as a witness that man's
condition, without a turning of the will that cannot come
about by any ordinary process, is miserable and desperate;
this truth, not his errors, does most to make him hated.
Like Balaam, he wished to curse but was compelled to
bless; wishing to oppose Christianity to the knife, he bore
valuable witness to a vital, but in his time already neg-
lected, Christian truth.

The example of Schopenhauer shows how false it
would be to hold that the doctrine of Original Sin is a
piece of absurd tradition, which you can believe only if
you are either brought up to believe it or, as a convert,
accept it as one part of the religion to which you convert;
a doctrine for which there is no evidence worthy of
consideration in the real world. For Schopenhauer accepted the doctrine not as implicit in Christian faith but on
its own account, taught as he supposed by Oriental lore;
and he showed that there is all too much evidence for it
in the human condition.

Original Sin

One thing Schopenhauer brings out is how an apparent change of character may conceal the same old ruling passion, in eighteenth-century terms, merely pursuing its goal by different paths. Humanly speaking, the will is unteachable, *velle non discitur*. Again, how often an agreeable middle-aged man or woman becomes intolerably selfish in old age! Schopenhauer would say: it is not that character deteriorates with age; the evil will was there all along, masked with polite pretences; with senile decay of the intellect the bad will has merely revealed itself as it was all along. This fearful thing does not happen to men solidly rooted in the love of God. We may remember the traditional story of how the Beloved Apostle, when he had no strength or wits left to say anything else, still kept repeating 'My children, love one another.'

What then must we conceive the state of man before the Fall to have been? Scripture tells us little, only that God made man upright and happy, and that if man had stood in this estate he would have lived for ever. There have of course been many theological speculations. For one thing, man's powers of intellect before the Fall, and his actual endowment of knowledge, have been greatly enlarged in theological imagination: an Aristotle, it has been said, was but the ruin of an Adam. We need not, I think, believe any such thing; we may be content to believe that Adam knew enough to serve God and live the kind of life God had made him for; if he was tending a garden, as the story has it, he would not need to know the ins and outs of Aristotle's syllogistic.

C. S. Lewis, who has valuable things to say in his book

The Problem of Pain, does not indulge in this sort of fancy – indeed, to my mind he is, on the contrary, too ready to picture Adam as a slow-witted savage resembling the traditional cave-man – but has a fancy of his own, that in unfallen man those bodily functions which in us go on automatically, and without our awareness unless they are going wrong, were subject to conscious control. I can see nothing in Scripture that supplies the most tenuous foundation for this, nor does it appear reasonable. Why should conscious control of these processes be anyhow desirable? I am well content to leave my liver alone so long as it leaves me alone; why should it have been otherwise with Adam? In the Hindu religion, the ability to play tricks with the functioning of one's body counts as a sign of high spirituality; but Christian spirituality has never had such a tradition. We need believe no more on this matter than that in unfallen man the body's functions were wholly subservient to mental life: it would not have been, as it is with us, that fatigue, disease and old age should drag the mind down so that its performance of ordinary necessary tasks is impaired, let alone its freedom to contemplate God.

God made man upright: man's will was oriented towards God in loving obedience; man's animal impulses were firmly under control of his will; man's understanding, whatever its limits, was surely free from the distracting fancies, prejudices, and superstitions that afflict us all – Bacon's idols of the tribe, the cave, the theatre, and the market-place; man's body was the unhindering instrument of his mind. From this good estate, man fell by pride and disobedience: he wanted to be like God, decreeing for himself what is good and evil. (In ever so many academic moral philosophers of today, this alleged right to decide standards of good and evil by one's own authority is upheld under the title of 'autonomy'; a grossly fallacious argument is put up that passes from the triviality that 'My decisions are my decisions and I accept the standards I do accept' to the falsehood that 'I cannot, or should not – it is not clear which! – accept standards set by some outside authority.' But I cannot dwell on this sort of academic folly here: I have said more about it in my book *God and the Soul*.)

With the good order of man's internal polity overthrown in the mutiny of its ruler (Lord Willbewill in Bunyan's parable of the Holy War) the consequences were, as Lewis insists, not a matter of arbitrary penal infliction, but simply of God's not intervening to prevent what was otherwise inevitable. Aversion from God, who is Truth, meant that man's mind became clouded with all manner of errors; and the animal appetites and bodily functions of man, no longer subject to a will that served God, went their own way as they do in the lower animals. Man having lost understanding became as the beasts that perish, liable to their uncontrolled passions, and to their mortality.

For our first parents, this rebellion in the house of life will have been unspeakably grievous. To find a hand striking in anger, or legs running away in fear, before the rational mind had time to act; to learn by painful self-discipline to restrain these irregular movements; this will have seemed to them no less pathological than when

95

(as occasionally happens) a mental patient's hand ceases to be under his conscious voluntary control but, for example, writes automatically words for which he is not consciously responsible. To us, their fallen posterity, such irregular motions are all too natural. For the root of evil is not in the disorderly passions, but in the will, perverse from our infancy up, that readily accepts the way we are as the way we ought to be. The will does not merely yield in the struggle or get taken by surprise: it positively identifies itself with perverse desires, and thereby makes them still more perverse.

This holds good in particular for two sorts of desire: erotic and combative. We learn from Scripture that disorderly erotic desire followed immediately upon the Fall. (It was not, as is sometimes represented, by sexual sin that Adam and Eve fell; they had been commanded to increase and multiply, and the disturbances by which they knew they were naked *followed* the Fall.) And the first man born into the world to a mother was the first murderer. In our times it would be idle to cite the abundant evidence for man's lechery and murderous cruelty. It is easy to see how shallow is the explanation of this as a trait surviving from man's brutish ancestors, which we may hope will be got under control by further evolution. There is not the slightest evidence in the course of history that man's lechery and cruelty are diminishing. Nor can animal ancestry be blamed; the great apes, our alleged cousins, rarely kill one another; war, as opposed to individual fights, is an unknown thing for them; and men are enormously more lustful than apes. It is not that desires shared with lower animals corrupt man's will; his already corrupt will corrupts his animal instincts, and makes them assume forms of monstrous excess and perversity unknown in the animal world. It may here be worth mentioning a falsehood industriously propagated by the advocates of sexual licence: the theory that sexual indulgence will cut the roots of human aggressiveness in sexual frustration: 'make love, not war'! History abundantly shows that lechery and cruelty can very well flourish together; it was so in Pagan Rome; it was so again in old Mexico, where the traditional religion required human sacrifice on an enormous scale, ritual cannibalism, and ritual sodomy.

Original Sin in us is not constituted by depraved sexuality; but Christian tradition has consistently held that our sexuality is specially infected by Original Sin. By the act of generation, which in no man is fully under control of the will, Adam's undying germ-plasm propagates itself; and his perverse will still lives on and reincarnates itself in a new human individual, who by nature will want to be the sort of creature a fallen man is, not the sort of creature God made Adam at the first. For this situation, within the resources of human nature, there is no remedy.

It is against this sombre background that the good news of Redemption shines out gloriously. I said before that without the doctrines of the Fall and Original Sin in their uncompromising traditional form the Christian message is so radically altered from what it once was as to lose all credibility. I can now spell this out more clearly: to alter the story of what man has been redeemed from is to abolish the old concept of Redemption, and therewith to reject the Christian faith altogether, at least by implication.

It is not my task here to expound the doctrine of Redemption: I can make only a few points. First, the doctrine of Original Sin makes intelligible the need that the Redeemer should be born of a virgin: not of the will of the flesh, nor of the will of man, but of God. Those who have abandoned the doctrine of the Virgin Conception do so only when they have anyhow abandoned the doctrine of Original Sin and therewith the doctrine of what the Redeemer came to remedy; with this last step, though they may still profess the Christian name, their apostasy from Christianity becomes manifest. For the heart of the Faith is the belief that Jesus is the Christ, the Son of God; people who deny the Virgin Conception never are found to believe that he is the Son of God in any but a distorted sense. This is the faith that Mary accepted from the lips of the angel when he told her how her Son should be conceived; this is the faith of Peter, against which the gates of hell shall not prevail.

Schopenhauer saw the congruity of the doctrine: for him, alas, God was a delusion and Christ a myth, so for him the Virgin Conception was only a telling metaphor for the new birth that some men experience, he could not tell how. His realization that man cannot be saved by any intellectual knowledge but only by conversion of the will unfortunately led him to hold that the Christian belief occurring in the converted was only an irrelevant bit of nonsense in their heads, whereby they sought to conceptualize the peace that passes all understanding. It reminds me of what a friend of mine once said: 'It

98

doesn't matter what you believe, so long as you're in-
sincere.'

My friend's idea was that a man of good heart may not
be much harmed by believing all sorts of nasty nonsense,
so long as his belief is a matter of notional not real
assent (to use Cardinal Newman's terms). There is
something in this, but we need to go carefully. First,
we should not too readily conclude that a man has a good
heart: certainly not, from his avoiding trouble with the
civil law and being well enough liked by his neighbours.
(How mistaken this is was in fact emphasized by
Schopenhauer.) Secondly, a notional belief is like an
unexploded bomb; so long as it is there in the mind,
we never know when it will explode into real assent,
though lapse of time may make this less and less likely.
In particular, it is not safe to suppose that somebody's
notional assent to Christian doctrine that is authentic in
its content will not suddenly explode into real assent
when the moment of truth comes and he has to choose
between apostasy and martyrdom. So from his own point
of view a worldly man should not be content to say of
another 'Of course he's a Christian, but he's all right – his
heart is in the right place.'

Indeed, there was some truth in the insulting description used by Pagan Romans for Christians, 'enemies of
the human race'. As regards any individual unconverted
man, to be sure, Christians can only desire that he should
be saved and come to knowledge of the Truth. But what
they want him to be saved from is precisely that natural
condition of mankind which the will of unconverted men
massively approves. 'Christians,' the worldly man must

think, 'are deserting the ship, and causing alarm and despondency among the sailors by spreading the report that she is sinking; their treason is none the less heinous because the ship to which they are trying to desert is only a ghost-ship.' Authentic Christianity must then at bottom be odious to the worldly man. (It is otherwise for the 'Christianity' of those false prophets who in the name of God and Christ promise the ship a prosperous voyage and a safe harbour, and urge Christians to work loyally upon her, to advance her trade. Far as he was from the Kingdom of God, Schopenhauer was nearer than these men.)

It must always be remembered that salvation is individual. Just as there is a fashionable doctrine of collective guilt, so there is a doctrine that men have been collectively redeemed. But that is equally false with the other doctrine. Collective salvation could be accomplished only if God reversed time and undid the sin of Adam; but it is really nonsense to speak of that. The race stemming from Adam is like a tree. In view of the continuity of germ-plasm, this is more than a metaphor. Think of a banyan tree: it sends down trunks from its branches that take root and branch and then more trunks grow down from these branches and so on. Each of us similarly grows out of the cell-division of that undying germ-plasm; and in each of us, as I said, the same perverse will reincarnates itself. The tree is diseased, root and branch. In it and for it there is no hope at all. Only by being grafted into the new life that came with Christ can individual members of Adam have any hope of life. And this must happen for each man separately. I have always remembered a Christadelphian friend in a lecture asking, 'How narrow is the gate to eternal life?' and answering 'Just wide enough for one person at a time.' Though entering the gate leads you to the glorious company of Christ and the Saints and Angels, you must enter alone. If you want the pleasures of following a leader in a crowd, there is a broad and easy road for you, but it leads to destruction; solidarity with mankind at large is something a Christian must renounce once for all.

This is the Christian story of Fall and Redemption. Some of the facts to which it draws our attention are grim; but the *Outline of History* story of steady upward progress from ape-man to cave-man from cave-man to barbarian, through Egypt, Babylon, Greece, Rome and medieval Europe to the glorious light of modern civilization, is a story in the end incredible and leads to utter despair. It proved so to H. G. Wells himself, who at the end of his life wrote a little book called, significantly, *Mind at the End of its Tether*. Man is a god who has failed; but there is a God who has not failed, and who offers each of us – in the words of Robert Roberts – 'godliness for manliness; life for death'.[1]

[1] *Christendom Astray*, Free Library Edition (London: Frank Jannaway), p. 329.

6

THE ORDAINER OF THE LOTTERY

The problem of evil is not some lofty abstract speculation, like the speculations about the expanding universe
and black holes; it concerns us all to think about it. For
men have to fight against evil, and there is no discharge
in the war; anyone who thinks he can enjoy life and
opt out of the war is a deserter. Of course I am not
saying that every man has to envisage some particular
evil and fight against that all his life; some men have
that vocation, but not all; many men best combat evil
by promoting some positive good in their own neighbour-
hood. Not everybody has to fight evil in the same way;
but nobody can buy himself out of the armed forces.
Now the strategy and tactics we employ in this war will
be sound *only* if we have a true view of what is our
actual situation and what possibilities are really open to
us. The point of any serious discussion of evil is to aim
at getting such a view. Some view we shall certainly
have, true or false; *il faut parier*. Nowadays a man may
high-mindedly bring up his children to decide for themselves whether any religion is true and whether chastity,
courage, and truthfulness are to be practised: of course he
does not try to persuade them in the matter, he fairly
presents the arguments on both sides. Such a man is not
being neutral about whether there is a God who com-

mands us to be chaste, brave, and truthful; he is betting his life – and so far as in him lies his children's lives too – that there is no such God who will judge him.

A mischievous cant of the day would have us think we are all responsible in a measure for all the evils in the world; I remember someone arguing that television, which brings the sight of the world's evils into our homes, has greatly increased our responsibility for them. It is impossible for anybody to take this cant really seriously – else he would go mad with grief and frustration – but the result of it is that men are hindered from doing good and curing evil where they best could; instead they divert money and energy to dubious distant enterprises, and indulge in futile bellyaching. 'The eyes of a fool are in the ends of the Earth.' I once read a story about a Jewish family in the United States: the son was burned up with a sense of guilt for what 'we' had done to the Negroes; the father retorted that the family had come to the States, to get away from pogroms, long after Negro slavery was abolished; that neither he nor his fathers had ever enslaved Negroes; and that whatever his son might feel about it, he himself had no intention of letting Gentiles slobber off their guilt feelings all over him. Only the doctrine of collective responsibility could make one deny that the Jewish father was right; and I have argued already that the doctrine is contrary both to Divine revelation and to good sense.

A true view of the problem of evil is needed for us to avoid false guilt feelings – God knows any of us has a lot of real guilt to worry about! – and to keep off campaigns that are futilely misdirected or worse. For example, concern over the pain of animals can lead us into foolish actions if *phronēsis*, practical wisdom, does not regulate our natural sympathy with beings with whom we share our animality. Apart from feeble attempts to restrain the predatory instincts of cats, I imagine nobody has been foolish enough to plan how men may reduce the pains sub-human living creatures inflict on one another. Such pains belong to the order of nature that is woven in warp and woof on the loom of predation and parasitism; and I have argued that such an order of nature can be regarded as God's work and casts no shadow of doubt on his perfection.

People have vehemently maintained that we should not torment animals with experiments or kill them for food. On the first point, as at present advised, I think that English criminal law draws the right line: there is nothing necessarily wrong with research that involves inflicting pain on animals, but in view of human corruption a legally unrestricted power to inflict pain would often lead to atrocious cruelties. (On the other hand, it is merely comic that the RSPCA should have threatened a man with prosecution for teaching a snail to drink beer; perhaps the society thought his action likely to deprave and corrupt young people who saw the snail's performance.) On the second point I have no hesitation at all. There is no shadow of a reason why human beings should not kill animals for food, unless we were to believe in metempsychosis, in the passing of an identical soul or self from human to animal bodies. In my book *God and the Soul* I argued that there was no reason to believe, and no clear way to understand, even reincarnation in a new human body; metempsychosis is much less intellectually acceptable.

The Judaeo-Christian tradition is unequivocally committed to the lawfulness of eating animal food. The Jews sacrificed animals in the Temple, and regularly ate their flesh; so far from making any departure from this tradition, Jesus Christ chose fishermen as his Apostles and helped them with their work, and instituted the memorial feast of the Last Supper after celebrating the Passover with a slain lamb. St Paul tells his converts to eat whatever they find in the butcher's shop and not trouble their consciences about it (1 Cor. x.25). To maintain that abstinence from animal food is even an ideal, let alone a matter of obligation, is plainly contrary to Christian thought.

The more fashionable 'thou shalt not' is that it is wrong for us men to disturb the balance of Nature. I am not sure what the balance of Nature is supposed to be or why it should be wrong to disturb it; but if men are to have roads, towns, and agriculture, they will certainly cause much disturbance to the species in the environment; without roads, towns, and agriculture on the other hand our life would become poor, nasty, brutish, and short, and I have not heard of any conservationist who urges that we should abandon these means of civilized life for conservation's sake (nor should I readily believe in his sincerity if he did so urge). I have read a conservationist lamenting that wolves and bears no longer run wild in England; perhaps if they did, this would in his eyes have the added advantage of checking the growth of population. As I remarked, however,

conservationists' hearts do not bleed for *Rattus rattus*; not
that *Rattus rattus* is at the moment a 'threatened species';
rats are a threat to us at least as much as we are to them.
I am not saying that men have an unquestionable right
to destroy other life for their own ends; they may well
be harming their fellows and robbing their children and
grandchildren; men of any generation are only life-
tenants of the Earth, and they have to reckon with
the Landlord if they waste his goods. But the charge
of 'disturbing the balance of Nature' is a piece of absurdity.

In regard to the evils of our own condition, the primary
issue is whether the doctrine of Original Sin is true. If it
is not true, then perhaps there is a hope that 'These
things shall be, a loftier race' and all that; perhaps the
present wickedness and misery of man is due to the
System – parents and teachers, in the present version of
the story, play the villain-parts formerly allotted to
kings and priests – and a new System with proper
education will produce a wiser and happier generation.
But our view will be quite different if we believe that
each new generation is born with a flaw for which there
is none but a supernatural remedy, and that in this life
even that remedy can effect only a partial cure of each
individual; we shall then have much less sanguine hopes
of what we can do for the betterment of human life. We
shall act like doctors whose patient is chronically ill with
an incurable sickness, and attempt no more than palliative
treatment of the symptoms. The more ambitious a
scheme is for the benefit of mankind, the more sceptically
we shall regard it; the more the scheme presupposes for

its working large-scale wisdom and self-control on man's part, the more certain we may be that its promises are deceptions.

The grim facts that Christians ascribe to Original Sin are written in history in letters that who runs may read; the corruption of man's heart has often been recognized by non-Christians, even by men extremely hostile to Christianity; to man's own folly and wickedness the greater part of man's miseries may clearly be traced, and this source of misery is not going to dry up till Kingdom Come. Does 'till Kingdom Come' here mean 'till the Greek Kalends', or 'till we all blow ourselves to Kingdom Come'? or does it rather mean 'till He shall come whose right it is'? This is not a philosophical question. But it is reasonable to hold that there could be a remedy for our ills if and only if man had a Ruler who knew the remedies and could enforce their application in spite of any resistance ('rule thou in the midst of thine enemies!'), and with regard to whom we need not fear either that absolute power would corrupt him or that his death would leave us with an unworthy successor. Such is the traditional Judaeo-Christian Messianic hope; if it is vain, there is no hope for any radical improvement in the human condition. Some people wish to say, it appears, that because the Christian Church exists, this age in which we now live, viewed with the eye of faith, *is* the Messianic age. I can only echo some words of Schopenhauer: if this were not mere thoughtless mouthing, it would be an indescribably wicked mockery of man's ills.

That even in this world human wickedness meets with

natural penalties, manifest and grievous, constitutes no sort of argument against the goodness of God. What does create a problem is the very unequal distribution of suffering. One man sins and suffers, another to all appearances escapes the penalty of his misdeeds; much suffering too comes upon one man by the misdeeds of another, whether this suffering is inflicted by the male-factor's will and act or simply follows as a consequence. On top of this, there are the cruel sufferings that come upon men from unforeseeable natural disaster and from accidents and diseases that were humanly unavoidable. The just and the unjust suffer alike. With complete impartiality, the infection may strike the city councillors who let the sewerage go wrong, the men who are doing their best to put it right, and the children who had no knowledge or responsibility in the matter.

Indiscriminate bombing is often condemned: and rightly so. People who try to defend it can do so only by dulling their minds with some variety of nonsense: about the collective responsibility of the enemy popula-tion, or about the bomber's not needing to *intend* the massacre (he may adroitly 'direct his intention' some other way), or about the 'incarnational' attitude that readily accepts the need to choose between sin and sin in this sadly imperfect world. But if we condemn indis-criminate bombing, does not the world-order so to say bomb us men indiscriminately? and how then can we regard it as the providential order of a Just and Merciful and Almighty God?

To this question Thomas Hobbes toughly replied that almightiness was a sufficient justification for God's infliction of pain upon innocent rational creatures: such infliction no more raises a problem than the pains of irrational creatures, which cannot sin. This doctrine may well appear repulsive: all the same, I think it is nearer the truth than some alternative answers I shall consider.

A view of the matter that Christians continually slip into (and that Hobbes flatly opposed) is that a man's misfortunes are regularly to be regarded as a 'judgment' upon him. The explicit words of Jesus Christ against the idea that the collapse of the tower of Siloam was a judgment upon the people who happened to be there when it fell are far too often forgotten by his disciples. One of the painfully comic episodes in Edmund Gosse's *Father and Son* is the description of how his father, Philip Gosse, wrestled in prayer to find out for what particular sin a particular misfortune of one of his flock, say a broken leg, must be deemed to have been a punishment, and how he resolved this hard matter to his own satisfaction.

To be sure, Holy Scripture sometimes explicitly states some apparent accident to have been a divinely appointed punishment, as when the lion slew the prophet who had disobeyed the word of the Lord (3 Kings xiii.23). But this would be matter of explicit revelation: Christians have been too prone to think that the thing speaks for itself. Yet if a man's misfortunes result from his misdeeds, and that as a *per se* consequence and not *per accidens*, then we have reason to call this a Divine judgment upon him: as Hobbes would say, to the Law of Nature there are annexed natural punishments. The greedy courtiers of Henry VIII who had seized upon the confiscated estate of St Thomas More were themselves executed for high treason a year or so later: that was the natural penalty for courting a tyrant and thereby making themselves ready targets for his murderous caprice. It is like Robert Louis Stevenson's fable of the two friends: 'And you took him for your friend? said the Judge. My good fellow, we have no use here for fools. So the man was cast into the pit.'

There are other cases in which a man's misfortunes seem appropriately linked to his crimes: the Jacobites made much of the fact that William of Orange died from falling off a horse that had formerly belonged to Sir John Fenwick; Fenwick having been beheaded after an Act of Attainder rather than a proper trial. But even if we granted to the Jacobites that Fenwick was unjustly put to death, it would be quite unwarranted to call William's dying this way a punishment. Riding accidents occur to good and bad men alike, and deaths from this cause are distributed, as we shall see, not according to the principles of vindictive justice, but only according to what are called the laws of chance.

Another answer to our problem, sometimes put over with a great deal of *pathos*, is the neo-Stoic doctrine that no evil can befall the just man; what are vulgarly regarded as evils may befall him, but for him they are not evils. This doctrine is buttressed with the idea that 'harm', 'injury', 'damage', are not properly descriptive terms but evaluative ones: it all depends on our values how we apply them. But I do not think a judge trying some prisoner on a charge of inflicting grievous bodily harm either would be or ought to be impressed by a plea that it depends on a free choice of values whether we count blinding or maiming as being harm at all; counsel would not have the nerve so to plead.

A case that keeps being mentioned in this connexion is Brentano's: allegedly Brentano said he welcomed the blindness that came upon him in later life because it enabled him to concentrate on philosophy instead of suffering the manifold distractions forced upon him by his eyes. The story naturally arouses sympathy for a brave and unfortunate man, but we should not let our tears fog the lens of philosophical consideration. Would Brentano actually have refused a surgical cure of his blindness? and ought he to have? *Per se*, blindness is certainly an evil even for a virtuous man, for it must seriously restrict his power of exercising his virtue; and as McTaggart remarked, a virtue that is indifferent to the ill-success of its endeavours is scarcely consistent.

I know nothing of Brentano's life and character, and I wonder whether those who cite the case know much more; we should need to know a great deal more in order to be certain that it is wrong to allow Brentano's alleged remark to remind us of certain fables in Aesop: The Fox and the Grapes and The Fox who Lost his Tail. However that may be, let me take a case of which I know a little more: the historian and philosopher Collingwood discovered that he was suffering, not from some disease or defect that would leave the intellect unaffected, but from a degenerative disease of blood-vessels in the brain, which made him less and less capable of doing any good work. Under this threat, Collingwood bravely worked as he could while it was day; will our neo-Stoics say he ought not to have regarded the threat as an evil?

Yet another attempted solution that I have come across is the Calvinist solution that Jonathan Edwards puts forward in his book on Original Sin. I have spoken of innocent sufferers; Edwards simply denies that any sufferers are innocent; on the contrary all men are sinners and deserve the unending pains of Hell, and it is mere mercy on God's part if some of us are let off. Even the pains of little children, Edward argues, afford us no reason whatsoever for hoping that in an after-life some recompense will be made to them; on the contrary, little children are a generation of vipers under the wrath and curse of God (apart from a few elect ones); their sufferings in this life are a mere slight foretaste of what will happen to them for ever hereafter, and to us too if we are not converted; and God is very merciful in giving us this warning, and in cutting the children's life short before they had committed worse sins and deserved more grievous damnation.

Plainly we have here Edwards at his very worst; but even at his worst he often has something to teach us. For he did not err in sombrely depicting the great evil of Original Sin, but in not seeing the generosity of Divine Grace, which freely offers to every man – though in this life we do not see how – a genuine chance of salvation from this intolerable burden. And Edwards is right too in insisting that our sin is not just a matter of individual voluntary acts of wickedness, but also of a radically perverse set of the will; such a perverse set, so far from making men's sin less detestable, makes it more so.

Edwards can fairly claim that this is the teaching of Scripture: it is also the teaching of human reason, if not corrupted by sophistries, as we may see in Aristotle's doctrine that the *akolastos*, the chronically vicious man, is worse than the *akratēs*, who lapses into wrongdoing through lack of self-control.

The world lies in wickedness. Because of Original Sin itself, and because of foolish plans that do not take this grim fact into account, even what seems done with good will is often disastrous; still more what is done with conscious bad will. As regards those of us who have come to years of discretion, only he who swims deliberately against the stream of the world can hope to be saved. Saved from what? The doom of a will alienated from God is a natural, not an arbitrary, penalty. For it is not by an arbitrary decree or out of petty possessiveness that God has made the rational creature incapable of permanent happiness except in the knowledge and love of God; it could not be otherwise – God, who unites all truth and beauty in himself, is the only *possible* source of such happiness. The natural penalty of a will self-alienated from God is the extremest misery.

As regards us adult human beings, it is a needless question whether God can justly afflict the innocent: we are not innocent, we are guilty. Some of us have a will alienated from God (a fact of which the comforts of life may make us blissfully unaware); such men have no complaint against God for the severest possible evils of this life, for it is a mere mercy of God that they are not suffering even more and suffering without remedy. Others of us have converted towards God, but how halfheartedly! how gladly we would be at home in Vanity Fair! and then for us suffering is a necessary medicine to cure the remaining disease.

The best of men suffer too. For them, as for Christ their Master, suffering is not merely penal or medicinal: they gladly accept it as what shapes their souls into immortal diamond. It is not possible that their souls should be so shaped without such afflictions; the virtue would not exist without the suffering. I have heard an anti-Christian philosopher maintaining the contrary: that a man could be, for example, highly courageous even though his courage were not tested by enduring any affliction or danger or even the appearance of danger; God, if he is almighty, could simply *make* men's souls to be such that *if* there ever were any danger or affliction they *would* react courageously – and this would be making them courageous. How reasonable this contention is I must leave my readers to judge.

But I must return to the problem that those human beings who by reason of age or mental defect are incapable of personal sin nevertheless suffer; and that both for them and for others the allocation of good and evil fortune follows in general no discernible principles of distributive or retributive justice, but simply the laws of chance.

What are the facts? We have an *a priori* idea of what a pure chance distribution would look like and we find this pattern over and over again in the allocation of good and evil fortune. During the years 1875 to 1894 German cavalrymen were kicked to death by their horses in a statistical pattern corresponding to our ideal of pure chance; as if in every year each cavalryman had drawn for tickets in a fair lottery, and a certain number of the tickets were marked for death by a horse's kick within the year.[1] A gentle-hearted Quaker, Lewis Richardson[2], conducted an elaborate statistical analysis of outbreaks of war and returns to peace; but the temporal pattern of these 'deadly quarrels', as he preferred to call them, again turned out to be purely chance; it was as though the matter were decided in the way a Greek poet might fancy – by the Father of gods and men drawing lots for peace or war from urns standing beside his throne. A similar urn model gives us the pattern of deaths in an epidemic; this time it is as though whenever a black ball for death were drawn, several more black balls were put in before the next draw.[3]

Is this seeming reign of chance compatible with Divine Providence? Some Christians regard any resort to chance with extreme aversion; I have never understood why. I remember a newspaper report of a Council meeting: two councillors were proposing to settle amicably by a toss-up which should be the next year's Mayor, and a minister of religion who was of the Council walked out sooner than countenance such ungodly procedure by his presence. Clearly he did not know his Bible very well, or he would have recalled that a similar procedure was used to

---

[1] J. M. Keynes, *A Treatise on Probability* (Macmillan), pp. 401–3

[2] *Statistics on Deadly Quarrels* (London: Stevens, 1960), pp. 128–42

[3] Richard von Mises, *Probability, Statistics, and Truth*, pp. 204–6

decide which of two worthy candidates, St Matthias and
St Justus, should be an Apostle in place of Judas Iscariot
(Acts i.23–6); and that was rather more important than
who should be next year's Mayor. And I dare say he
did not give real assent to the doctrine that all events
however trivial fall within the ordering of Providence.
The lot is thrown into the lap, but the way it falls out
is from the Lord (Proverbs xvi.33). And this is the real
meaning of Christ's words about the fall of the sparrow.
It is false sentiment to picture God as concerned and
pitiful for the sparrow when it falls: my cat Smashhappy,
like the Psalmist's lion, seeks his meat from God, and if
it is to him the sparrow falls, that is Providence too. But
no detail of the universe is too petty for the Divine
knowledge and will; and we are of more value than
many sparrows. Like the pieces of a house that is to be
demolished only to be rebuilt, the hairs of our head are
all numbered.

This only shows, someone may object, that observing
the manifest chanciness of the world is psychologically
compatible with a belief in Providence, it does not show
the belief is reasonable. I grant the objection; for at the
moment I was only concerned to show that his view of
chance events as coming under providential ordering is
not some new speculation of mine but simply part of
Jewish and Christian tradition. But we should see already
that there is not here even an apparent contradiction to
overcome. If events really are chance events, that only
means that they are not predetermined by created causes,
not that they escape from the knowledge and control of
Divine Providence.

The Ordainer of the Lottery

Our naive notion of chance is certainly a bit vague, but it can be given precision and mathematical form. We naively apply the notion of chance to such classes of events as accidental deaths, the fall of dice, infection in an epidemic; with more sophistication, we have the idea of variously likely alternatives that ought to be proportionately often realized – and this idea we can apply, over and over again, in the real world. Pascal's calculation explained the experimental results reached by the Chevalier de Méré in his gambling; that was the start of the mathematical theory of probability. We should here notice an important source of confusion. Applying the theory of pure-chance patterns to (say) the falls of a certain die has no necessary connexion with the die's being 'fair'; even if the chance of a six is not $1/6$, we can still work out, given the chance of a six on a single throw, what is the chance of getting at least one six in four throws. Conversely, each side could come up equally often and the pattern not be a chance pattern at all; this is obvious, for we might have 1,2,3,4,5,6, 1,2,3,4,5,6 ... *ad infinitum*.

Chance conceived as the proportionate realization of variously likely alternatives excludes definite predetermination of the issue by factors already existing in the created world. The belief that such predetermination is universal – now more commonly held by philosphers than by men of science – appears to me a mere superstition. People will often say that of course any so-called chance event could have been predicted, though in practice the observation and calculations required would be too laborious:

The Ordainer of the Lottery

The method of this I would gladly explain
While I have it so clear in my head
If I had but the time, and you had but the brain. . .

Ever since Queen Victoria's reign this has been the theme of what may be called scientific sermonizing by men like Huxley and Tyndall and Clifford: high time the bluff should be called. Anyone who finds the word 'bluff' offensive should recall that Tyndall for example claimed to *know* that the weather is 'in principle' predictable, although *we* know that he had not even an inkling of the theoretical concepts by which the weather is at present (none too accurately) predicted.

The existence of statistical patterns of contingency does not exclude voluntary control of the course of events by God or man. The phonemes I utter, the letters I write down, conform to all sorts of statistical regularities; my freedom of speech simply rides upon these regularities, for they nowise suffice to determine what I say – truth or falsehood, sense or nonsense. And since any singular issue is compatible with any statistical regularity, it is not excluded that God, say in answer to prayer, should fix the issue of some contingent future one way rather than another. I have elsewhere argued (in the essay 'On Praying for Things to Happen', in *God and the Soul*) that unless you are asking for a miracle you can sensibly pray only about the way some future contingency shall go. For unless it is sometimes true that God brings about the course of events in a way that he would not had he not been asked, petitionary prayer is idle; just as it would be idle for a boy to ask his father for a specific birthday present if the father has made up his mind what to give irrespective of what the boy asks. And if the course of events may go this way or that according to what is asked of free choice by the petitioner, then it is contingent.

Contingency in the physical world is a necessary condition of human freedom. A man is not free unless some observable movements of his body are up to his own decision; so he is not free if his movements are predictable from some set of factors in the world that can be specified in a way that takes no account of his decisions. A man is not free in speaking if some set of causal factors that takes no account of his mind and will in speaking suffice to determine what sound-waves issue from his lips; he is not free about smoking, given that cigarettes are within reach, if causal factors quite apart from his own thoughts and intentions guarantee that his hands will pick up and light cigarettes and his lungs inhale and exhale the smoke. It is mere bluff, as I said, to pretend that such predictions as these are already feasible; it is a mere impious hope to say that they will become feasible when we know a bit more science.

At this point it is often objected that a freedom which consists in our actions being chancy and unpredictable is not something we ought to hanker after. I concede the point but I deny its relevance; for what I am arguing is not that macroscopic physical indeterminism is a sufficient condition of human freedom, but that it is a necessary condition; the examples of the speaker and the smoker point up the incoherence of the Leibniz–Pope position about Almighty God, which

The Ordainer of the Lottery

binding Nature fast in fate
Left free the human will.

If men are to act freely there must be both some deter-
minism and some indeterminism in the world. As
Austin Farrer argued, men would not be capable of free
action if all their instruments and the materials they
acted upon behaved with individual capricious ways: we
should be in the predicament of Alice trying to play
croquet with live flamingoes for mallets and live hedge-
hogs for balls. But equally we could not play croquet if
the ball and mallets moved and impinged on one another
as the stars in their courses, in a way that could be predicted regardless of the rules of the game or the
players' aims.

Our freedom is our supreme dignity; that makes us
children of the Most High; we can enjoy it only by
living in a partly chancy world – and that means a
world in which there will be goods and evils of fortune
distributed according to the laws of chance. We have
no choice but to enter for the lottery; and we are able
by taking thought to learn its terms; for the Ordainer
of the lottery, as Thackeray called God, both gives our
minds the idea of chance distributions and lets us find
many clear examples of them in the world. We cannot
opt out of the lottery nor alter its terms; and it is vain
to look *here* for distributive or retributive justice; it is
only that the Ordainer of the lottery plays fair.

I am of course not denying that God does manifest
retributive justice; even in this world we often see
natural rewards or penalties ensuing upon obedience or

disobedience to the natural law, and in the next chapter I shall argue that the pains of Hell too are a matter of God's allowing the natural penalties to take their course rather than of ingeniously appropriate vengeance. But in this life the good and evil dealt out only with the fairness of a lottery very often overshadow these natural rewards and penalties.

God's distributive justice certainly does not consist, and could not possibly consist, in his rendering equal good to equals. All that any man has and is is a free gift from the God who freely made him; it is sheer nonsense to fancy some antecedent status of equality that could be regarded as even conceptually prior to God's gifts. All are men and as such have certain common rights to consideration from their fellows; but men are manifestly not equal, and to say they are equal in God's sight is profane clap-trap; it is as when Mr A and Mrs B, ignoring Mrs A and Mr B, say they are married in the sight of God. It is no less absurd to rail against God for making men unequal.

Nor does human inequality extend only to this life. There is no reason to believe, and Christian tradition has never taught, that God gives all men an equal share, or even an equal chance of an equal share, of grace and glory. It has sometimes been held that God distributes his graces according to his foreknowledge of who *would* use them best if given them; but this rests on a picture of Divine foreknowledge that would be quite untenable if what I have already argued in this book is correct. But it is part of Christian faith that every human being without exception – though it will take Judgment Day to show us how – receives a genuine chance of attaining to the unspeakable Glory of the Divine Life, and can forfeit this only by his own ill will; and if this is so, then nobody is in a position to complain that God's ways are not equal.

7

HELL

The Scottish Shorter Catechism begins with this sublime question and answer:

Q.   What is the chief end of man?
A.   The chief end of man is to glorify God and to enjoy him for ever.

The dogma of Hell is the doctrine that by sinful choice men may finally fail to achieve that chief end, and that such men are in consequence irretrievably miserable; moreover, that this misery never comes to an end in a final destruction of the wicked.

We cannot be Christians, followers of Christ, we cannot even know what it is to be a Christian, unless the Gospels give at least an approximately correct account of Christ's teaching. And if the Gospel account is even approximately correct, then it is perfectly clear that according to that teaching many men are irretrievably lost. Men like McTaggart and Bertrand Russell have noticed this aspect of Christ's teaching and decided that Christianity is incredible; they have thus paid Christ the minimal honour of observing what he has said and taking it seriously – an honour denied him by those who use their own fancy about the 'spirit' of Christ's teaching as a means of deciding what Christ must have said or meant. It is less clear, I admit, that the fate of the lost according to that teaching is to be endless misery rather than ultimate destruction. But universalism is not a live option for a Christian.

We cannot think properly about Hell if we do not start from a right view about God. God has no need of us as we need him; no need of us, or of our love. People have vainly fancied that God needed to create the universe so that he might have other persons, however inferior, to love and be loved by: much as a lonely old woman might crowd her house with cats. McTaggart indeed rightly remarks that it is difficult to regard personality as possible without an Other; but for a Christian this need is fully met in the eternal love for each other of the Divine Persons in the Blessed Trinity. In orthodox Trinitarian theology each Person is *alius*, somebody else, to the other two; each is *I* to himself and *thou* to the others –'Thou art my Son, this day have I begotten thee.'

God has no need of us, and our love of him is perverse if we wish God were otherwise. Spinoza was right in what he *meant* when he said that he who loves God does not try to make God love him in return; for in Spinoza above all men we must look at the proof if we want to understand what is being proved, and Spinoza's reason (*Ethics* v.19) is that a man who loves God can be conscious of enhanced perfection from thinking of God, but God who is unchangeable cannot be conscious of enhanced perfection from thinking of the man who loves him; nor, as Spinoza says, can a true lover of God *wish* that God could *gain* joy from the lover's existence, for so to wish is to wish that God were not God. And though the language would be different, this thought is to be found in the great Doctors of the Church – in Augustine and Aquinas and Anselm – as well as in Spinoza.

God does not need us; but that does not make God selfish in his attitude towards us; the question of his being selfish or unselfish does not arise. As Hobbes puts it, God has no ends; God is not a man that he should seek to increase his influence by getting men's worship; God cannot exploit us, for he has nothing to gain from us. On the other hand, as I said, God cannot wish us to have permanent happiness that does not depend on him; it would be unselfish for one human being to wish this for another, but in God the wish would be self-contradictory.

'This is just the way the rational creature was made' says Aquinas: 'to act for the sake of his end is within his free choice'. God chose that we should be free, even if it meant that many of us would reject God and be miserable: even if for many of us that misery would be unending. It is not for us to say that God has got his priorities wrong, and ought rather to aim at the greatest happiness of the greatest number; of course nothing in the world suggests that God has any such aim, either for beasts or for men; but to indict God for this is only a shade less foolish than to praise him for aiming at such a goal, for this idea of a goal is incoherent, as McTaggart pointed out. However many people there were, and however happy they were, they could all be happier, and there could be more of them. 'The greatest happiness of the greatest number' or 'the best of all possible worlds' is a piece of just such absurdity as 'the greatest proper fraction' or 'the most sinuous possible curve'. The phrase is no doubt useful in political speeches, but it has no place in philosophy or theology.

It is no discredit to God if some creature falls short of its end, its chief end: nor even if very many creatures so fail. The teleology of the reproductive apparatus in living things is obvious to any unbiased mind; only in the extreme folly of an intellectual fashion could men accept the explanation that species which by chance had such a complex mechanism survived, while others that lacked it perished. But most of the creatures so produced perish before maturity; in all such cases the chief end is not achieved. They do not therefore exist in vain: even we men can sometimes see how their existence subserves the general order of nature.

Wicked men, who by their own choice fail to achieve their chief end, nevertheless have their place in the Divine order of things. Spinoza said 'The ungodly, like tools in the hand of the Artisan, serve unwittingly, and in serving they are consumed'; and of course the Prophets of his own people constantly use this language. But we must here imagine that a chisel volunteers to be used to hack the wood, in the fatuous malicious belief that the carver is thus enabled to do harm to the wood. Extreme villainy is the necessary means to produce such virtue as that of Thomas More or Maksymilian Kolbe: necessary, because the virtue is exercized in reaction to the villainy, the villainy is the subject-matter of the virtue. God allows the villainy in order to have the virtue; and again it is not for us to say he has the wrong priorities.

Hell

God has no need of us; but we are lost without him; for we are weak and foolish and full of greed and hatred and we are visibly making a terrible mess of our affairs; humanly speaking, the race may well destroy itself, and in any event each of us has to die. If this were all, we could still praise God for his great glory: for being there, for being God. Anaxagoras told the Athenian court that condemned him to death 'God condemned both you and me to death long ago'; but Anaxagoras also thought it was worth while to live in order to see the heavens and the order of the world, and to contemplate that Mind which established this order, whose knowledge and power are unlimited, which cannot be changed by anything in the world. And this is how we ought to feel, even if God were going to cut short our days and end them like a tale that is told.

For us, I believe, it will not end this way; the Christian Church promises that we shall rise from death in our bodies and thereafter die no more. Apart from that promise, which our Faith teaches us is God's promise, it appears quite unreasonable to expect any after-life at all; I argued this matter in *God and the Soul*. Resurrection is in any case a merely gratuitous gift of God. A race of rational creatures to whom this gratuitous gift had not been given might well be mortal and perish permanently at death; God would not thereby default on any implied promise to them or in any other way be acting unjustly.

I have sometimes wondered whether we have not some slight evidence for the perishing of such non-human rational beings. I once read a popular scientific article which argued that a bomb containing a modest quantity of a known radioactive element, if fired into a star like the Sun, would turn the star into a supernova by setting up a chain reaction. I cannot vouch for the science of this, but perhaps this is how supernovas do, very rarely, come about: that upon some planet sin-ridden like ours, a crazy war leader chooses this end for himself and his race when his defeat appears certain. What I want to emphasize is the moral that if a world perished thus, and all its inhabitants were as if they had never been, it would be nothing against the glory of God. For God a billion rational creatures are as dust in the balance; if a billion perish, God suffers no loss, who can create what he wills with no effort or cost by merely thinking of it; the perishing of those who break his Law is the natural penalty of their folly and can only redound to the praise of his Eternal Justice.

Must we then hold that, after all, the pains of the lost do end in annihilation? This view has been held by some Christians; but the weight of Christian tradition appears clearly against it, and in what I shall say henceforth I shall assume that it is false. I shall rather try to show that the final triumph of good and elimination of evil need not be regarded as incompatible even with the unending suffering of the lost.

I shall not discuss the intermediate state of souls between death and the Last Judgment. The only rational ground for a hope of immortality, as I have said, is the possibility of accepting the revealed doctrine of resurrection. I do not wish either to deny or to explain away the traditional doctrine that between death and the final resurrection there is a partial survival of a man as a separated soul; in fact I sketched in *God and the Soul* a defence of this dogma's credibility. I cannot now say much about the matter: Scripture and Christian tradition tell us little about the condition of separated souls, and I do not know that reason can determine much either. But like Aquinas I hold that there are difficulties in accepting the *sempiternal* existence of separated souls.

I of course do not mean that in itself the doctrine of resurrection appears reasonable on the evidence: quite the contrary. From time to time persons describing themselves as 'thoughtful' write to the newspapers to point out that if a body is destroyed by fire or devoured by wild beasts there is a difficulty in seeing how it can rise again. A 'thoughtful' person in this connexion is a person who has taken enough thought to see that something is a *prima facie* objection to the Faith, but has not thought enough to consider the likelihood that believers have thought about the matter during the last nineteen centuries. Of course in Nero's time, or Antiochus's for that matter, it was obvious even to the least thoughtful believer that his body might be burned or devoured; he believed in his own resurrection, not because this looked empirically likely, but because he believed his God had promised it. A Jew under Antiochus remembering the three boys in Nebuchadnezzar's furnace, or a Christian under Nero thinking of the Resurrection of Christ, need have no doubt that God could and would perform what he had promised.

We are not to perish; we are to rise again and live for ever. How is 'for ever' to be understood? At this point

I expect the protest to arise in some minds that I am thinking in terms of endless time and not of eternity. I reply that whenever a modern writer about religion starts speaking of eternity I expect him to fall into nonsense. I have already argued against some illegitimate ways of speaking of God's eternity.

I must now return to the topic because it is by the sense in which eternal life is ascribed to God that we must understand the eternity of Heaven. God's eternal life was characterized once for all in the phrases of Boethius, which mortal man cannot better: it is *without terminus*, either first or last; it is *enjoyed completely and all at once*, not bit by bit like our life. Imperfect as our understanding must be, we can and must avoid two opposite errors. On the one hand, we must avoid thinking of God as an abstract thing like a number, which has no life and can bring nothing to pass: God is infinite activity, and his duration embraces and overflows all duration in time. On the other hand, we must not ascribe to God changes on account of what happens in his creation. Eternity in this sense -- active unchanging life without beginning or end -- belongs to God alone.

When a creature is said to enjoy eternal life, we must mean that somehow it shares in the Divine life; but we lack the means to imagine such felicity. Our felicity in this life is, as Hobbes put it 'continual success in obtaining those things which a man from time to time desireth'; a life in which there is no antecedent desire and hope for the good, and no fear of losing it either, is beyond our comprehension. 'What kind of Felicity God hath ordained to them that devoutly honour him, a man shall no sooner know than enjoy', says Hobbes: and I can say no more. But it is anyhow clear that this felicity cannot be timeless; we certainly do not enjoy it now, and we hope by God's mercy to enjoy it in the future.

The only philosopher that I know of who has tried in a serious way to explain how Heaven can both be timeless and yet be rightly spoken of as future is McTaggart. He ascribes to every person the eternity and blessedness that Christians ascribe to God; but he holds that in many (perhaps all) persons there *coexist* with that blessed state states of misperception which are variously evil and miserable. The Heavenly state and the states of misperception together form a non-temporal series, which is misperceived as a time-series; and in that series the relation that generates the appearance of earlier and later really hold from states of this life to the Heavenly state, no less than it holds from the experiences of hearing a lecture today to the experience of breakfast tomorrow. So just as even McTaggart, who denies the reality of time, will speak of tomorrow's breakfast as future in ordinary conversation, so also we may conveniently call Heaven future.

McTaggart's philosophy, which I have just sketched, is open to many objections; but I think he is right in claiming that only his philosophy can make sense of regarding Heaven as future and yet as being really eternal. And that philosophy is fundamentally atheistic: for I have argued that denying the reality of time is fatal to theism, as McTaggart himself argued. So a theist, who rejects McTaggart's philosophy and affirms the reality of time, cannot regard the joys of Heaven as properly eternal. At most there will be some level of experience in the Blessed which is immune from change and fear of loss and is a changeless enjoyment of God; but this blessedness will have had a real, not just an apparent, beginning in time. There is no reason to believe this means that the life of the Blessed ends in a state that is wholly changeless; nor is it at all traditional so to believe. One of the gifts ascribed by Scripture and tradition to the Blessed in the resurrection is agility – the power to travel quick as thought wherever they will; such a power has no meaning in a terminal state of changelessness.

Again, it is traditionally held that Christ our Saviour was *simul viator et comprehensor*; that throughout the struggle and suffering of his earthly life his soul was at some level resting in the arms of his Father in perfect peace. The congruity of this doctrine should be apparent from what I have said before. If the doctrine is true, then Christ's recorded claims to teach with absolute authority and command our assent are justified: he is speaking of what he sees and knows. If the doctrine is false, then Christ was walking in ignorance and hope like the rest of us; people might be right in ascribing to him, as people nowadays do, utter *faith* in his Father and his mission; but why should we believe him, when he himself, the source of Christian faith, just *believed* and didn't know? So it is almost impossible to accept Christ's authority and *not* believe that in his earthly career he enjoyed eternal life and the vision of God. But if so, eternal life for a man will certainly not necessarily exclude a series of varied experiences.

Hell

We thus have no reason whatever to ascribe even to those who enjoy eternal life the attainment of a state beyond all time and change. There is still less reason to ascribe any such thing to the damned in Hell. If at one level of experience there is an unchanging beatific vision of God for the Blessed, that is no reason at all to believe that an unchanging miserific vision of the Devil is one level of experience for the damned in Hell. (The phrase 'miserific vision' comes from no traditional source, only from C. S. Lewis; and to my mind it is one symptom of a slight Manichean strain in his thought, like his idea that the development of predatory and parasitic animals is the work of the Devil.) Boethian eternity can be ascribed only to God; a creature's share of eternity can only be a share in the life and happiness of God; the Devil could not have Boethian eternity, nor could the other damned share in his eternity by sharing his misery. Hell is not Heaven reflected upside down in a black mirror. Hell is eternal merely in the sense that it goes on and on and never stops: literally, Hell is one damned thing after another. Endless duration in time may stagger the imagination, but I believe it affords no difficulty for the intellect; the arguments against its possibility appear to me patently fallacious.

Does a dogma of Hell make unacceptable an alleged Divine revelation which contains the dogma? I shall argue that it does not. I am not concerned at this point to expound or to defend the idea of Divine revelation, nor yet to discuss in general what considerations ought to weigh with us in estimating the claim made for an alleged revelation. Still less am I concerned to argue positively in favour of the Christian claim. All that I shall argue here is that although the existence of Hell would be a very terrible thing, it is neither incredible that there should be a Hell nor any reproach against God that he should inflict Hell upon the wicked, and that there is no good reason to reject traditional Christianity merely because the dogma of Hell is part of the tradition.

In any case, the mere frightfulness of Hell is no ground for not believing in the possibility of Hell. Many frightful things do happen. Christianity is often supposed to be a matter of wishful thinking; but the accusation can scarcely hold good against a Christian who firmly accepts the dogma of Hell, and believes that he and those he loves, just as they may die of cancer, are in jeopardy of Hell. But Hell is not just a disaster that men may have to face; Hell is supposed to be inflicted by God. If the infliction of Hell could rightly be regarded as wicked – and if so, it would be enormously, unimaginably wicked – then we could reject the dogma of Hell with a good intellectual conscience: not because it is too bad to be true, but because there is not the faintest possible reason to believe it.

As before, I acknowledge a debt to McTaggart. The logical strength of McTaggart's argument (*Some Dogmas of Religion*, §177) is rather hard to judge coolly in the original form, for he stated it in a way highly offensive to pious and gratifying to impious ears: so I shall restate it in my own way. There is no ground in natural reason to believe in Hell; people do believe in Hell only because the existence of Hell is a revealed dogma, and people have grounds for believing in Hell only if such a dogma's being revealed is ground for believing it. What now needs to be shown, and I think can be shown, is that if the infliction of Hell is very wicked, then there is no reason to believe the revelation telling us that there is a Hell, and thus no reason to believe in Hell after all.

Let us suppose that the infliction of Hell is very wicked but that there is a revelation telling us that a supreme being does inflict Hell. If the revelation is true, then the supreme being is enormously wicked. Let us then call him not 'God' but 'Ahriman'. If what Ahriman's worshippers tell us is true, Ahriman's character is vile; in that case it is childish folly for them to accept his assurances as to the conditions on which they may avoid Hell – Ahriman, if he is as wicked as all that, may be quite capable of amusing himself by sending people to Hell after all, when in the hopes of avoiding Hell they have degraded themselves by flattery of Ahriman all their lives and denied themselves pleasures that Ahriman forbids. So if the Ahrimanian creed is true, then it is quite irrational to worship Ahriman or obey his alleged commands, even in the hope of saving our souls from Hell. But further, if the Ahrimanian creed is true, then it is quite irrational to believe it is true. If we did believe it, we should be trusting the alleged word of Ahriman: and that a being capable of unlimited cruelty and injustice is to be believed on his mere word, with so much at stake, is too ludicrous a proposition to need discussion.

This argument appears to me convincing. McTaggart made it harder to appreciate its force by calling the supposed wicked supreme being 'God'; the gratification that this would cause to an impious reader, or the horror it would cause a pious one, is something of an obstacle to cool logical appraisal. But I do accept the argument and its conclusion: if the infliction of Hell would be wicked, then there is no reason to believe that such infliction occurs.

It follows that I have to show that the infliction of Hell is not wicked, if I am to show that the existence of Hell is not incredible. And again it follows that some forms of the dogma of Hell really are incredible. Predestinarian theories like those of Jonathan Edwards would be an example. It would be unspeakably wicked to make men's performance of certain actions causally necessary, and then torment the men everlastingly as a punishment for having performed them. But as I said before, predestinarianism is incredible even apart from its dogma of Hell; for it would make God directly responsible for the lies men tell in the same way as for the utterances of his holy Prophets, and thus the revelational basis of the belief is wholly destroyed.

'The good old gentleman', Thomas Hobbes, thought a predestined Hell for predestined sins utterly incredible, and sought refuge in a doctrine of the annihilation of the wicked:

it seemeth hard to say, that God who is the Father of Mercies, that doth in Heaven and Earth all that he wills; that hath the hearts of men in his disposing; that worketh in men both to do, and to will; and without whose free gift a man hath neither inclination to good, nor repentance of evil, should punish men's transgressions without any end of time, and with all the extremity of torture that men can imagine, and more. (*Leviathan*, c.44)

Hell

Since men had been burned for heresy in Hobbes's lifetime, I see no reason to doubt his sincerity when he puts forward arguments for the deviant sort of Christianity that he professed; a secret infidel would rather profess the local orthodoxy with all its most repellent doctrines, and make their repulsiveness come out by innuendo:

> Damn with faint praise, assent with civil leer,
> And without sneering teach the rest to sneer.

So I do take Hobbes's theology seriously; but I do not think he can save predestinarianism. I imagine he would react to my argument that predestinarians would make God the author of human lies, as he did react to the general objection that if predestinarianism is true God is the author of human sins: by saying that we are not to say anything about the matter. If the next step in an argument would lead to a monstrous false conclusion, one must indeed come to a halt; but then one should retrace one's steps and try to find what has gone wrong. Hobbes went wrong, I think, about human freedom. And Hell is certainly not justly inflictable on beings who lack freedom of choice. A man lacks freedom of choice if the way he acts is causally necessary given some factor or factors that are wholly outside his control. He may feel free to choose in that case, but his freedom will be illusory. Whether Hell is justly inflictable on beings who have freedom of choice is a question that still remains to be examined.

I am not defending a doctrine of Hell in Dante's style as the arbitrary infliction of ingeniously contrived appropriate torments; God is not, to my mind, like Gilbert's

Mikado. But God does allow men to sin; and misery is the natural, not the arbitrarily inflicted, consequence of sin to the sinner. God is the only possible source of beauty and joy and knowledge and love: to turn away from God's light is to choose darkness, hatred, and misery. God is not like a jealous parent resenting his children's seeking happiness outside the home; apart from love for God men can find only misery, in this world or in any conceivable world; and God could not make men so that they did not need him. Nor is God's will and purpose frustrated by those who cast themselves away. In this life this wickedness serves to perfect the virtue of God's friends; hereafter, the misery that comes from their evil will serves for the praise of God's justice. God has never promised to make all men happy: on the contrary, as Butler argued in the *Analogy*, the lesson that a man may by his own foolish choice do himself irreparable harm is written in this world in letters that he who runs may read. Immortality accompanied by vice is, as Aristotle said, the greatest of misfortunes.

Nor is the quality of life in Hell beyond our understanding like the blessedness of Heaven. When a man is dying from senility or some terminal illness, he sometimes shows himself as prey to the most violent evil passions: terror, despair, rage, hatred, malice. The spectacle is so fearful that lover and friend and kinsman cannot endure it: 'This is not the man we know', they will cry helplessly, and they will desire nothing so much as the person's death so that this may be at an end. The story is put around (as I should say, put around by man's enemies) that this is just a natural result of physical

138

deterioration; but that is just a lie; as I said before, no such thing happens to those whose hearts are firmly fixed in love towards God. But it need not surprise us if this dreadful thing happens to a man who has hitherto been an agreeable companion after the fashion of this world. Up to now he has worn a mask; now senility has robbed him of the skill of holding the mask in place, or utter weariness and despair make the pretence seem no longer worth while; and the Hell that burns within him becomes visible.

People say rather lightly that they could not bear for a damned soul to be punished unendingly; but someone confronted with the damned would find it impossible to wish that things so evil should be happy – particularly when the misery is seen as the direct and natural consequence of the guilt. At best they could wish that such a thing should no longer be; that such guilt and misery should no longer defile the world. About the possible gratification of this wish I shall have more to say in a moment. But if we imagine any hope of conversion excluded, love and pity for a damned soul are as manifestly excluded as they were in fact found impossible by the man's nearest and dearest in the terrible cases I have mentioned. Here, I believe, God shows us what Hell is: though there are those who will not be converted though one rose from the dead.

It is worth saying at this point, against certain Protestant theologians, that the pains of Hell that I have just been talking about cannot have been part of the Passion of Christ. Whether Christ's cry of dereliction from the Cross corresponded to a temporary loss of the Beatific

Vision I should not like to say; but we may be certain that Christ never felt these pains of a frustrated evil will, for his will never was evil.

The argument against the perpetuity of Hell that seems to me to have most weight is one that has nothing to do with any wish that sinners should in the end escape punishment by extinction; and still less with any idea that all men have a right to be happy. It is rather that the work of the Divine Artist would be permanently marred if the surd or absurd element of sin were a permanent element in it. And though Scripture is full of places that offer no hope to wicked individuals, Scripture also holds out the glorious vision of a world in which sin and death are finally banished and sorrow is a thing of the past; so I should say that this argument can claim some Scriptural support.

After the general resurrection, Judgment; *krisis*; the final separation of good and bad. I shall try in the remainder of this chapter to sketch speculatively how this separation may be so conceived that we understand its being final and irretrievable, and how we can nevertheless understand and accept the idea of a world completely purified and made new. The foundation of what I say is to be sought in what I said before about time and the future. Time, I argued, is badly, misleadingly, represented by a single line, whether the model does or does not include a point moving along a line. For there are alternative future possibilities, and before the event none of them can be known as *the* future. God indeed can give someone the gift of prophecy; but the prophet is declaring what God decrees shall happen, not what God somehow sees as happening; and any prophecy still leaves much open. To someone who says that this makes God's knowledge of the future very restricted, I reply that God both knows all possibilities of development and has complete control over what actually happens, and that as regards what actually happens God's knowledge *is* his power: *scientia Dei, causa rerum*. I should admit that my account made God's knowledge limited only if I had to ascribe to God such things as surprise, frustration, regret, and improvisation: but of course I deny that I need ascribe them to God.

If time is represented by a line, the line must fork. It can fork towards the future, but not towards the past: just as our action can alter the future, but not the past, so there can be alternative futures, but not alternative pasts. So if the line of time splits anywhere, the split halves never join up again: if they did join up, there would be alternative pasts at the point where they did join up again.

I suggest that the *krisis* of the Last Judgment consists in the realization, from then onwards, of two alternative futures for the world into which saved and damned alike rise again. What happens to the saved after the Last Judgment thus stands in no time-relation to what happens to the lost after the Last Judgment. The just cannot properly then so much as ask what the wicked are doing *now*; or the other way round. The proper tense for either Heaven to use about Hell, or Hell about Heaven, is the past future tense: it was going to be. The saved can say 'There was going to be Hell': the damned, alas, can say 'There was going to be heavenly bliss'. The Day will make it unambiguously clear to each and every man that God has not been unjust; that for each man there was an open road to Heaven; that if he is now lost, it was his ill will that made him miss the right turning. Contrariwise, the Blessed will see how narrowly they escaped taking the wrong turning, time and again. (That, as the Saints have said, is what the Last Judgment is for.)

Of course the infernal line of development for the future would not be a future world including *only* the damned, nor would the celestial counterpart be a future including *only* the saved. Various physical objects, such as the terrestrial globe and the heavenly bodies, might be expected to figure in both alternative futures; and the future history of one and the same body would therefore split in two. Is this logically possible? I have already explained that I am excluding, I think on good logical grounds, the joining up again of lines of futurity that have once split; and if this is excluded, the realization of *both* of two alternative futures for one and the same body does not seem to involve insuperable logical difficulties. Since the whole of this is a speculation, it would be an inordinate use of space to go into the logical problems in detail here; but I may mention Arthur Prior's paper 'Opposite Number' (available in his book *Papers in Logic and Ethics*, Duckworth, 1976) for a formal argument to show that at least the most obvious attempts to refute this suggestion of split futures turn out to rest on uncertain assumptions or invalid reasoning.

In rejecting the idea that the separation of Heaven and Hell is spatial, I may seem to lay myself open to the charge that I claim to know better in the matter than my

Lord and Saviour; people can hardly help remembering the parable of Dives and Lazarus. But this parable is not a theological account of the state of the dead, even though Aquinas read it that way when he was writing the *Sumna Theologica*. I have heard that medieval inquisitors condemned the Talmud for irreverent stories about God; I cannot help suspecting that they were unfair – after all it was not Rabbi Akiba (let us say), but Rabbi Joshua ben Joseph, who in parables compared God once to an unjust judge, and once to a young rake who stays out to all hours and beats his servants if they dare to snatch some sleep before his return. The parable is a Jewish story, and to understand it one needs to know the genre. Our Lord was using popular Jewish notions of Abraham's bosom and Gehenna, but not thereby vouching for their truth; the point of the parable was the last sentence – that people who are not converted by the Law and the Prophets will not be converted though one rose from the dead. (And in fact many people were not converted when One did rise from the dead.) If we are to take this parable as straightforward theology, then we might as well conclude from the parable of the Unjust Judge that in ruling the world God has no regard to justice but will grant sufficiently persistent demands so as not to be further pestered.

In saying that Christ taught the irretrievable loss of many men, I was of course not relying on this parable at all, but on frequent and explicit words in the Gospels. When this chapter was to be delivered as a lecture and was announced, somebody asked whether I believed in Hell as people believe in New Zealand. Alas, so far as I can foresee I am much more likely to end up in Hell than to visit New Zealand. But perhaps the point of the question was different: *Where* do I think Hell is? I have tried to explain that I think of Hell not as a place but as a possible future. I have remarked elsewhere that phrases like 'the next world', 'the other world', 'the world to come', have suffered a curious semantic change: they used to mean a new age of time, that which will succeed the Last Judgment – *vitam venturi saeculi* – but have come to mean another world somehow elsewhere, like Mars or the Moon. Similarly people think of 'the end of the world' as a destruction of this globe, perhaps of all the material universe; but the phrase properly and traditionally means the end of the age, and medieval thinkers still believed that this Earth is not to be destroyed but renewed and glorified on Judgment Day. The second Epistle of St Peter says that one age ended with the Flood and ours will end with fiery destruction of man's works; well, the latter is quite easy to believe without revelation. It takes faith to believe that after the Day that burns like an oven there will be a new age of justice. But not all men will be counted worthy to live in that age: for the damned, I have argued, there is another future.

When I thus deprecated thinking of Hell as a place, I was not speaking of *present* damnation for separated souls or lost angels. But since they are *ex hypothesi* immaterial, no place can be straightforwardly ascribed to them; and their damnation is in any event a state not a place. As Mephistopheles said to Faustus's question 'How comes it then that thou art out of Hell?': 'Why, this is Hell, nor am I out of it.'

Hell

Let us then consider first what on this view will be the lot of the damned. For them, all love and joy and peace are things that were once, and were once going to be, but now will never be, never any more. For them, the Blessed and God's grace have disappeared from the world for ever. With no hope of death, they are left for ever with their own dreadful company. And they will be inescapably aware, as men in this world easily forget, that whether they will or not they must be subject always to the Divine Power; that they have shaken off their ease but not their yoke. Perforce they will accept God's Power, but being wicked they will not submit to his Justice; it will seem to them fearfully unfair – they will be like the brutal greedy poisoner who was dragged from the dock screaming 'Je demande la justice!'

The damned will know that there is no conceivable restitution for them. Time cannot run backwards to bring them back before Judgment Day; nor can their world ever become the world of the Blessed, for if it did it would become a world with two incompatible pasts. On this view, what separates Heaven and Hell is not gates of brass or chains of iron for the prisoners, nor yet a great gulf between; Heaven and Hell after Judgment Day are separated by the hard logical necessity that makes the past unalterable and irrevocable: a necessity that is not imposed upon God but is his very Truth and Justice.

So much for the essential pain of Hell, the pain of loss. But I do not doubt that there will be superadded to this a physical pain of sense, which will be an unremitting torment, and to which only the pain of a man burning in flames could be an adequate earthly comparison. I do not believe, as for example Aquinas held in a youthful work, that this torment will be inflicted by specially created fire with remarkable physical and chemical properties. The right view seems to me to have been formulated by Jonathan Edwards; and divined long before him by a wise heathen, Empedocles. We take it for granted, by use and wont, that the inanimate creatures should be subject to the perverse wills of sinners and subserve their wicked ends. We vaguely think, perhaps, that God is bound to let it be so if he is to rule the cosmos by law. We are wrong in our view of the matter. As I have said, the mere existence of sin is a mystery that God alone can see through. The subjection of inanimate creatures, whose sole *raison d'être* is God's good pleasure and God's glory, to the perverse will of God's enemies is not the course of nature, but a miracle of God's mercy and forbearance; to give the wicked time and opportunity to repent, and meanwhile to exercise the virtue of the just.

For the damned, after the Day, there will be no more forbearance; when they try to use the inanimate creatures (as they now do, defiling and plundering the Earth and abusing Nature for their wicked purposes) they will find that Nature at last manifestly obeys her Master and not them – and so the ordinary course of Nature will continually frustrate, enrage, and torment them: continually, because their will is obstinate in evil. For the wicked man, mere physical comfort will be as irretrievably lost as love and joy. 'For the mighty Air,' says Empedocles, 'drives him forth into the Sea, and the Sea vomits him forth upon the dry land; Earth tosses him into the beams of the blazing Sun, and the Sun flings him back into the eddies of the Air. One element receives him from another, but all loathe him.'

It needs no insistence to bring out how grievous on this view is the lot of the damned; by making their pains to be natural penalties of wickedness rather than arbitrary inflictions, I have not made them less terrible. It was not my aim to show that Hell was not utterly terrible; only to show that God is not unjust in respect of Hell. But nobody need incur such a grievous lot; anyone who goes to Hell will go because he spurned the Grace of God and chose evil rather than good, and Judgment Day will make it apparent that nobody can truly say to God – though no doubt the damned will still *say* – 'I never had a chance.' May my lot and yours be rather with those for whom sin and sorrow and folly are things of the past; for whom Hell is only a bad dream of what once might have been the future but can now never happen, not for evermore; for whom the wicked are nightmare figures vanished with the morning and will play no part ever again under the Sun. 'Yet a little while, and the wicked shall not be: you shall seek his place and it shall not be found. But the meek shall inherit the Earth: and they shall enjoy abundance of peace.'

APPENDIX

The speculation about permanently split futures for the blessed and the damned is not intended, nor do I think it necessary, for justifying the belief that Hell is both a possible state for men and one compatible with God's goodness. What I was trying to argue is that the fact of Hell may be compossible with the realization of the hope that one day all manner of things shall be well and sin and sorrow be banished from the world for ever. For this hope there appear some grounds in Scripture and the thought of the Saints.

The mode of reconciliation I have suggested commended itself to me just because the notion of a future that forks into incompatible alternatives is not brought in *ad hoc*, but already appeared to be required by the partial contingency of Nature and the freedom of choice in God and man. I stress once more that this is only a speculation; I do not purport to be expounding a dogma of Christian faith.

Nor is this the only speculative possibility of reconciliation. Imagine a man condemned to work out for ever the decimal expansion of π: a dreadful fate for many of us to imagine. He would always have a new digit to work out, however far he got, so his task would never end. But if he worked out the first digit in half an hour, the second in a quarter of an hour, and so on, his speed of calculation doubling each time, then if he started at two o'clock no digit would remain to be calculated after three o'clock. A corruptible human brain could not perform this feat; but as Bertrand Russell rightly said, the impossibility is only medical, not logical, and we need not suppose men after the resurrection to be subject to such medical impossibilities. So an unending series of miseries could be fitted into a finite time-stretch. In that case, a man condemned to Hell might look forward to a series of miserable experiences of which he could say with truth 'This will never end'; and nevertheless one day the Saints might be able to say of him and of all the damned 'Thank God that's over.'

INDEX OF PROPER NAMES

Index of Proper Names

Index of Proper Names